Adventure Racing

Adventure Racing

Jacques Marais

with Lisa de Speville

NH
NEW
HOLLAND

First published in 2004 by New Holland (Publishers) Ltd
London · Cape Town · Sydney · Auckland
www.newhollandpublishers.com

86 Edgware Road
London W2 2EA
United Kingdom

14 Aquatic Drive
Frenchs Forest, NSW 2086
Australia

80 McKenzie Street
Cape Town 8001
South Africa

218 Lake Road
Northcote, Auckland
New Zealand

ISBN   (HB) 1 84330 723 5
ISBN   (PB) 1 84330 724 3

Publisher: Mariëlle Renssen
Publishing Managers: Claudia Dos Santos, Simon Pooley
Commissioning Editor: Alfred LeMaitre
Studio Manager: Richard MacArthur
Editor: Roxanne Reid
Concept Design/Cover: Steven Felmore/Lyndall du Toit
Designer: Lyndall du Toit
Illustrator: Philippa Allen
Picture Researcher: Karla Kik
Production: Myrna Collins
UK Consultant: Ken Kissick, Chairman, Adventure Racing
Association of the UK and Ireland
USA Consultant: Don Mann, President, Odyssey
Adventure Racing

Reproduction by Hirt & Carter (Cape) Pty Ltd
Printed and bound in Singapore by Tien Wah Press (Pte) Ltd
10 9 8 7 6 5 4 3 2 1

DEDICATION

*To Ugene, Karyn and Craig, who tramped, cranked and bashed with
me during the Porterville Eco-Adventure Challenge, giving me my first
(and best) taste of adventure racing.*
                                                        Jacques Marais

Foreword

If you have picked up this book, you have somewhere, somehow been drawn to the challenge, the intrigue of the fast-growing sport of adventure racing. For those of us who are already fully immersed, somewhere along the line of our lives, adventure racing pulled us in – maybe from something we saw on television, an article we read, a friend who needed a teammate or support crew. But once it penetrated our skin, it was a matter of time until it seeped to our core.

Before I learned of the sport in 1993, I had never been on the seat of a mountain bike, in a climbing harness or crampons, carried a compass or hung by a rope. I did not own a backpack or kayak paddle. But it did not matter. From the first minutes I watched a report of the Raid Gauloises that year, a desire erupted in me for something bigger than myself, something larger than my life. Some people say that the more we become transfixed by the computer screen, and the more sedentary our lives, the stronger the physical voice within yearns to be heard. That small voice buried deep within me could not be ignored. With no experience whatsoever, I attended a tryout for an American team for the Raid Gauloises; in winning, a different life was created. Today, over 20 races and 10 years later, I have been able to live my imagination, my adventure fantasies and my dreams.

I am often asked about my best and worst races, my greatest racing accomplishments and biggest fears. Many times, they are one and the same. On paper, the achievements would read: winning the Elf two years in a row, consistently placing in the top three in all major events, maintaining competitive rankings in the Raid, Eco-Challenge, Southern Traverse and many others. But, in reality, the high points have been those races where, against all odds, we triumphed as a team.

In the 1996 Eco-Challenge in British Columbia, our team captain and another critical member quit the team a couple of weeks before the race. We met two new teammates, foreign to the sport, at the airport on the way to the start line. Without any experience together, our prospects were dim. But an immediate respect for each other and unusual team dynamics allowed us to straggle across the finish line in second place when only three of 74 teams actually finished the original course.

In the 1998 Raid Gauloises in Ecuador, I was personally thrashed. During the race, I had pulmonary oedema, severe bronchitis, a dislocated shoulder, separated AC joint, and to-the-bone hip abrasions. I felt like an anchor being dragged by my team. But the suffering motivated us to another level.

An unparalleled unity, a camaraderie birthed only by unbearable pain, allowed us a second-place finish in another race where only a small percentage of the competing teams crossed the finish line.

These experiences prove time after time that no matter how unlikely success may seem, no matter how grim the situation may feel, when you separate yourself from your own conscious, when you are part of something greater than yourself, anything is possible. This is but one of the lessons brought to life for me by the sport of adventure racing. Now that the sport is well known across the globe, there is a multitude of opportunities for you to live adventure racing, both personally and vicariously. Regardless of how competitive you are, it is always the combination of physical endurance, athletic skill, mental toughness, emotional flexibility and sheer drive to get to the next checkpoint that determines your success. From simply following the sport on TV or the Internet, to helping from the sidelines as support, to making it a weekend hobby, to adopting it as a lifestyle, the epic sport of adventure racing is guaranteed to excite and inspire you, and bring home to you the true meaning of adventure!

Cathy Sassin

Contents

Chapter 1: **The origin of adventure**   **8**
history, race pioneers, top international racers

Chapter 2: **The AR way**   **16**
what is adventure racing (AR)?

Chapter 3: **Thinking through the race**   **24**
planning, motivation, survival tips, race safety

Chapter 4: **Kit inspection**   **34**
gearing up, dress sense, the perfect pack

Chapter 5: **AR disciplines**   **46**
trekking, biking, aqua action, mountaineering, etc.

Chapter 6: **Tactics and strategy**   **82**
race briefing, combining disciplines, transition tips

Chapter 7: **Navigation**   **94**
map reading, magnetic deviation, route options

Chapter 8: **Support crews**   **106**
support dynamics, responsibilities, useful skills

Chapter 9: **Fuelling your body**   **114**
race food, energy boosters, supplements

Chapter 10: **Medical know-how**   **122**
first-aid tips for handling illnesses and injuries

Chapter 11: **Ten amazing races**   **132**
top races from around the globe

CHECKLISTS   154
GLOSSARY   156
FURTHER READING AND WEBSITES   157
INDEX   158

The origin
of adventure

THE IMPULSE TO EXPLORE new frontiers has been integral to the psyche of some humans since caveman days; some members of the clan would have gazed across familiar hunting grounds to undiscovered lands, itching to take up clubs and spears and set off on a bold adventure. On their return, they would have regaled fellow tribesmen with harrowing tales of charging mastodons or of the guttural roar of sabre-toothed tigers.

Later, military conquests saw armies marching onto new continents, soldiers, sailors and traders set forth on voyages of discovery, and burgeoning economies boosted travel. Africa succumbed to colonialism and American pioneers set out to conquer their brave new world. This unrelenting tide of explorers opened up new frontiers, sweeping ever further, deeper, higher. By the onset of the 20th century, few corners on Planet Earth remained unconquered by mankind, except the North and South Poles.

It was this formidable challenge that gave birth to a new breed of adventurer: the modern-day Polar explorer. The 'heroic era of exploration' during the early 1900s saw the emergence of many great adventurers in a race for glory that pitted men of exceptional endurance and mental strength against the harshest elements. Using crude equipment and basic

technology, American Robert Edwin Peary claimed the prized North Pole, while the race to the South Pole saw Robert Scott's and Roald Amundsen's parties go head to head in what could probably be

TOP AND INSET: One of the attractions of adventure racing is that it affords athletes the opportunity to visit some of the most beautiful corners of our planet.
ABOVE RIGHT: Explorer Robert Scott is honoured by a statue in Christchurch, New Zealand.

regarded as the first expedition race to captivate the attention of the world media. Global reporting saw polar devotees around the world avidly following the unfolding drama and final tragedy.

Fast forward to the next millennium, where passenger liners cruise the Antarctic and millionaire fat-cats wheeze to the summit of Everest by dint of a bevy of long-suffering porters. But even though civilization has tempered our immediate world, the spirit of adventure still burns brightly within many who continue to strive for their own first ascents or personal journeys of discovery. A tangible shift in how we communicate, travel, work, play and think has come about, opening new doors onto a world of adventure, and offering ordinary people an easily achievable adrenalin fix. Most importantly, adventure no longer happens at the furtherest reaches of our planet, but within our suburbs, cities or states. More people have more time and money to spend in the great outdoors, thus contributing to an adventure-sport boom. With edgy activities such as whitewater tubing, mountain biking, trail running, in-line skating and crossover mountaineering disciplines added to the mix, adventure junkies around the world suddenly find they are spoiled for choice.

Some athletes opted to combine various disciplines to maximize their outdoor pleasure. Orienteering and navigation soon blended with the action, resulting in an intriguing equilibrium between brawn and brain in a racing format that required strategic thinking, superhuman endurance and multiple skills. Cue to the birth of adventure racing, a brand-new action genre built around the concept of multiple sporting disciplines combined within a single event over a number of days.

The original expedition races

The origin of adventure racing may be traced back through triathlon to 1921, when the French initiated the Course des Trois Sports, or Race of Three Sports, combining swimming, cycling and running. More than 50 years later, the modern era of triathlon dawned with two Californian swim-bike-run events (Eppies and Mission Bay), before those seminal Ironman events were staged on the island of Ohau in Hawaii. A series of multi-sport races in New Zealand followed from 1980 onwards, with athletes competing in trail running, kayaking, mountain biking and alpine skiing in events such as the Coast-to-Coast and Alpine Ironman.

Approximately three years elapsed before the first extreme American race premiered in the outdoor arena – the no-frills Alaska Mountain Wilderness Challenge. Event organizers did not take long to cotton onto this exciting outdoor evolution, understanding that a multi-sport concept posed untold challenges to athletes in search of high adventure. Visionaries in this field include Gérard Fusil and Geoff Hunt, who initiated and facilitated growth of the sport by popularizing expedition racing.

In 1985, a company called Saga d'Aventures was created by Thierry Sabine (of Paris-Dakar fame) and Alain Gaimard to present the historic Raid Blanc event in the Alps. Illustrious French journalist Gérard Fusil lent his support and helped stage the first-ever Raid Gauloises in New Zealand in 1989, where 130 competitors took on a course combining 35km (20 miles) of trekking, 221km (137 miles) of rafting, a 60km (37-mile) run-and-ride (on foot and on horseback), as well as canoeing and rock climbing.

Beginnings in the United States

Adventure racing in the United States started in Alaska in the 1980s. There were few competitors, few rules, no dark zones, no insurance, no medical coverage, no publicity but a lot of real adventure. The guidelines were direct and simple: start at position A and race until you reach the finish line. Modes of travel were up to the competitors.

Then Mark Burnett took it a step further in 1995. Having competed in the Raid Gauloises in Borneo and Madagascar with three Navy SEALs who trained him, he saw the sport's television appeal and dropped out of racing to begin producing races. He recreated the Raid rules and format in New England and Utah, changing the name to the Eco-Challenge (*see* page 14). It was the 1996 Eco-Challenge in British Columbia with its high-profile television coverage that first really grabbed the attention of US adventure racers.

A year later, Odyssey Adventure Racing was created by members of Team Odyssey, one of the top US teams that had twice been the first-placed American team in the Raid Gauloises. After competing in the Raid in Patagonia in 1995, I believed I could design a race that could be completed in five days or less, and would be relatively inexpensive and accessible to almost anybody in North America. That is how Odyssey's Beast of the East (*see* page 134) was born in 1998.

When all my spare time was spent training team members, racing or designing training sites, it became time to formalize this training with the creation of the Odyssey Adventure Racing Academy later the same year. The Endorphin Fix, the toughest two-day race in the United States, was invented to test students finishing at the academy.

Proud to be purists rather than business people, driven by love of the sport and enjoyment of people who know how to push themselves and enjoy life, Odyssey now produces more adventure races, multi-sport competitions and training camps than anyone in North America.

Don Mann, Odyssey Adventure Racing

Today, the Raid has attained legendary status, pitting racers against the grimmest of elements in forbidding destinations around the world – from the desolate landscape of Patagonia and steaming jungles in Ecuador and Vietnam to the peaks of the Himalaya and the plains of Madagascar. The event is built on the concept of the total autonomy of racers within a natural environment, focusing on their ability to be singularly self-sufficient while at one with nature.

Although the rules may be modified to include traditional disciplines from a chosen race region, the basics remain the same: a non-stop race using only human (or animal) power from start to finish, via a range of checkpoints. Teams race at their own speed along a route planned by their navigator in order to pass through various compulsory control points. In 2003, the organizers adopted an X-Adventure Raid qualifying series, thus limiting entry into this celebrated event to teams who had proved their mettle during the qualifying series.

ABOVE: **Don Mann of Odyssey Adventure Racing is well known in the adventure racing world for his passion and commitment to the sport. As a race director, he is uncompromising, pushing competitors to the limit in exciting but gruelling events.**

During the 1990s, a number of other events joined the fray. Regarded by many racers as the toughest challenge in adventure racing (AR), one key event was the Southern Traverse, kicking off in 1991 with a 312km (194-mile) route through the brutal terrain of New Zealand's South Island. Rising levels of fitness and skills have seen race directors raising the bar, and today's events often take 10 days or longer.

Another was the Eco-Challenge, which is unmatched when it comes to media profile. Eco-Challenge director Mark Burnett saw the potential of an expedition race as a reality television spectacle and has, since his first race in Utah in 1995, built the event into an internationally recognizable brand. Television viewers around the world have sat glued to their screens, annually tuning in to man's struggle with the elements in destinations as diverse as Borneo, Fiji and Morocco. The race format remains standard, with teams of four adventurers racing 500km (310 miles) or more in a non-stop dash to the finish line. Only non-motorized modes of transport are permitted, with the route set between control points taking between six and 10 days to complete. Teams must finish as a unit, so illness, fatigue or injury to a single member would eliminate the team as a whole.

Despite constantly changing race formats due to a multitude of possible disciplines, one consistent factor sets adventure racing apart from most other sports – the environment within which these events unfold. Race destinations are selected for the challenges they pose to participants and the exceptional natural beauty of the region where they are presented. Participants must subscribe to a strong environmental ethic and anyone found transgressing ecological guidelines may face immediate disqualification or hefty time penalties. Social projects focusing on uplifting local communities are also favoured by organizers, with teams perhaps being asked to contribute books and clothing to aid projects or, in some cases, to assist in building bridges and clean-up operations, or in renovating school buildings.

TOP: **Mark Burnett, director of the Eco-Challenge, has done much to promote adventure racing as a high-profile sport.**

ABOVE: **A social project during the Eco-Challenge in Cairns, Australia, was to plant trees.**

The faces behind the races

Central to the sport are many legendary personalities, both competitors and race directors. Men like Geoff Hunt, Mark Burnett and Gérard Fusil have contributed enormously to the development of global adventure racing and have attained cult followings to match those of top competitors.

Fusil, an amateur racer and renowned outdoor journalist, is seen by many aficionados as the father of adventure racing. After working in New Zealand on a summer version of the Raid Blanc and witnessing the Kiwi Coast-to-Coast races, he decided to create a non-stop nature raid, eventually immortalizing this concept by presenting the first Raid Gauloises in conjunction with partner Alain Gaimard.

Fusil learnt much from the New Zealanders and it is therefore only fair to rate Geoff Hunt, race director of the Southern Traverse, as another founding father of the sport. As an accomplished racer with creditable finishes in the Raid Gauloises, Eco-Challenge, EMA and the Mild Seven Outdoor Quest, Hunt founded the world's second-oldest adventure race in 1991 (see 'The Southern Traverse: then and now' on page 13).

If Fusil is the visionary and Hunt the respected racer, Mark Burnett must be the master of media promotion. Not only has he conceptualized the Eco-Challenge and Survivor reality television shows, he is also a consummate producer with several Emmy awards to his name. Hearsay and rumour seem to beset him as an individual, but only the unenlightened will deny that this trendsetter has transformed the face of AR for the better.

As for the racers themselves, it is nearly impossible to choose a handful of heroes from a host of seemingly superhuman athletes. Some names do stand out, however, such as those of Petri Forsman, Cathy Sassin, Ian Adamson, John Howard and Rebecca Rush. Adamson, often billed as 'the world's toughest man', personifies the absolute adventure racer: an athlete of average height, lean physique, incisive mind, composed temperament and total lack of ego. Currently the cog around which Team Nike ACG/Balance Bar revolves, he has at times raced with 'The Three Goddesses', Robyn Benincasa, Cathy Sassin and Rebecca Rush, all awesome athletes in their own right. I met Sassin at the 2003 Global Extreme event presented in the Kalahari Desert in Southern Africa and, like every-one else, marvelled at her extraordinary poise, confident personality and well-toned body. Many of these stars of AR selflessly contributed to this book their personal advice and practical tips on choosing gear, training and racing. As you page through the book, their input will help you in striving to attain your personal potential.

Read on, learn and enjoy!

TOP LEFT TO BOTTOM RIGHT: **Geoff Hunt and Pascale Lore, Mark Burnett, Ian Adamson, Nathan Fa'ave, Robyn Benincasa and John Howard are among the many personalities who have made a significant contribution to the sport of adventure racing.**

The Southern Traverse: then and now

In 1989, Frenchman Gérard Fusil arrived in New Zealand with a wild dream to launch adventure racing – The Raid Gauloises, or Grand Traverse as it was called in New Zealand – onto an unsuspecting world audience.

As the most experienced Kiwi rafting guide, and owner of the Landsborough River Rafting Company, I was asked to assist as water safety officer. Soon, Kiwi competitors indicated they were keen to do such a race on an annual basis, so after two years of hard work, careful thought and meticulous planning, the Southern Traverse was launched in 1991.

The first course started at a remote lodge in the Southern Alps and raced toward Queenstown. Disciplines included rafting, mountain biking, road biking, and mountain running, with two crossings of high snowy passes. The fastest team, Doug Lomax's Team Designer Aluminium, finished the 312km (194 miles) in 40 hours and 57 minutes, with just three hours' sleep. Teams continued to finish over the next two days, some in better shape than others and all with stories to tell. One competitor commented, 'I think it should probably be described as an adventure rather than a race.'

The Southern Traverse, now established as an annual event with increasing competitor numbers, is today the largest race in the southern hemisphere and New Zealand's icon adventure race.

INTO THE FUTURE

The Southern Traverse, described by some of the early promotional literature as 'a sporting adventure race requiring endurance, resourcefulness and teamwork', was a hit with Kiwi adventurers. With our company's background in international competition, and a desire to challenge and satisfy racers, the early courses quickly earned the Traverse a reputation as an athlete's event. It has been called the toughest and most technical of all the big international events, although the courses have always been designed to include alternative routes for slower teams, so everyone has the chance to cross the finish line.

Initially, participation was primarily by Kiwi teams, but 1996 saw real international interest, with teams from the United States and Japan eager to discover what was making the Kiwis nearly invincible on the international circuit.

By 1998 the race had become, in Robert Nagle's words: 'The perfect length, long enough to require mental strength but not so long as to be physically debilitating.' Until 1999, it was based solely in the lower half of the South Island, but has moved around the Island since then. Future years could see it travel to the North Island or even further afield, but the vision will remain unchanged: 'To produce an adventure race we would want to race in.' And that may be one reason why it continues to attract the world's best racers.

Geoff Hunt, Southern Traverse

ABOVE: **New Zealand's South Island offers adventure racers from around the world a chance to pit their skills against challenging terrain, top Kiwi teams and a technical route designed by Geoff Hunt.**

History of the Eco-Challenge

The first Eco-Challenge, held in 1995 in southeastern Utah, was an exciting and somewhat mysterious event for most North American athletes. Apart from a handful of French, Australian and New Zealand competitors, few people had even heard of adventure races, much less competed in them.

This first race was a close replica of the French event, the Raid Gauloises, which was first held in New Zealand in 1989. In fact, the Eco-Challenge used virtually the same rulebook, including small details like a mandatory one-metre-long climbing rope for each competitor. No one seemed to know what this was for, but we had to carry it around the course nonetheless. In fact, it was in the Raid rules to secure a Petzl shunt to your harness as a backup for rappelling (abseiling).

Today, the Eco-Challenge has evolved into the world's best-known and highest-profile race, largely as a result of the media success of its owner and creator Mark Burnett. From humble and somewhat controversial beginnings in 1995 – when environmental groups protested against the race, inadvertently giving it much press attention – the event is now a television 'reality' show, part race, part media spectacle, and increasingly also an examination of the human condition.

With its big budgets and flashy presentation, today's Eco-Challenge has teams in five-star resorts, with dozens of camera crews and helicopters constantly buzzing the course. Despite its Hollywood shine, the race retains some of its original flavour as a long, tough and often punishing challenge for even the best adventure racing teams. Even the inclusion of movie star, television icon and playboy centrefold teams has not diminished its 'race' quality, and most athletes still regard the Eco-Challenge as 'the Big One'.

Ian Adamson,
Team Nike ACG / Balance Bar

ABOVE: **Ian Adamson dominates during a mountain-bike leg of the Eco-Challenge. One of the most respected AR athletes, he has often been nominated as 'adventurer of the year' in the United States and is universally known as the 'world's toughest man'.**

A winning mentality: AR in the Antipodes

New Zealand and Australia, revered internationally for their rugby and cricket prowess, are now staking their claim in the world of AR as well. This is not surprising, given their shared AR history, including such milestones as the world's first ever adventure race (now the Raid Gauloises) and consistent top-three finishes since the sport's inception.

Kiwis John Howard and Steve Gurney, and Aussie Ian Adamson, who is now based in the United States, are regarded by many as the top athletes in the sport, with the results to back it up. Furthermore, New Zealand has won more Eco-Challenges than any other country, with victories in Canada, Australia, Argentina and Fiji.

What makes the Kiwis and Aussies so good? Many athletes ascribe much of their success to the adventurous, dynamic outdoor lifestyle down under. As both countries are relatively young, people were until recently subjected to much hardship, extreme climatic conditions, variable bio-systems and long hours of work. The indigenous Aboriginal and Maori people added an element of their warrior culture to our psychological makeup, resulting in multi-skilled, adaptable athletes keen to take on any challenge.

Adventure is available in abundance, with superb rock climbing, mountaineering, wild rivers and oceans, mountain biking, impenetrable forests, caving, sailing, snow and ice. AR became a general extension of this. This is clear when you consider that in New Zealand, with a population of about four million, more than 90 per cent of people know what AR is and are familiar with not only the Eco-Challenge, but a range of local events such as the Arrow 24-hour series and the world-renowned Southern Traverse, regarded by aficionados as AR at its purest.

Neil Jones, one of New Zealand's top racers (together with John Howard) has won two Eco-Challenges and probably sums up the fiercely competitive Kiwi spirit best: 'For someone from New Zealand, the Eco-Challenge is the premier race to win, because it is the only race where you represent your country. And as everyone knows, we are extremely proud of our country and love flying the national colours.'

Nathan Fa'ave, Team Seagate

ABOVE: **Growing up in New Zealand moulded Nathan Fa'ave — and a host of other Kiwi athletes — into competitors with an adventurous edge. Here he competes in the roller blading section of the Primal Quest 2003 in Lake Tahoe.**

The AR way

WHAT IS ADVENTURE RACING, or AR? 'Insanity' might be the most common response to this question from a non-racing public, but tens of thousands of athletes around the globe will disagree vehemently. In answer, a basic summary may be something along the following lines: an adventure race integrates multiple disciplines in a single event, with teams

racing non-stop against each other and the clock, sometimes over a number of days. The race format will see teams navigating a series of checkpoints, using their feet and various other forms of non-motorized transport in order to reach the finish as a unit. Problem solving, strategic planning, teamwork and endurance are integral to AR and the events are usually presented within remote wilderness areas.

As you may expect of a young, dynamic and evolving sport, the nametag may vary in different parts of the world. Many Scandinavian countries, for example, refer to AR as multi-sport, while terms such as nature raids, off-road triathlons, cross-discipline racing, eco-racing, stage racing or expedition level racing pop up to describe respective genres of a sport incorporating anything from short-course and sprint races to multi-day, classic events.

How to get into the AR habit:

1	Get fit enough to swim 1km (½ mile), run 5km (3 miles) and mountain-bike 20km (12 miles) ✓
2	Sign up for an AR training camp or clinic ✓
3	Get a good book about AR, join an AR discussion group, chat room/Internet forum to pick up tips ✓
4	Volunteer as a backup crew member for an AR team to get a feel for the action ✓
5	Enter a sprint race lasting around three hours ✓
6	Enter an urban challenge event in your town/city ✓
7	Once you have completed a sprint event, try a short course or 'weekender' of 60–120km (37–75 miles), usually taking up from 24–36 hours ✓
8	Improve your base level fitness by working on your endurance training ✓
9	Watch the experts and talk to them to fine-tune your techniques ✓
10	Eat right – nutrition is as important as training ✓

Start a new way of life

If you are addicted to the great outdoors, an obvious entry into the world of AR would be to sign up for an adventure racing training camp. Usually, these

TOP: Sprint races, such as the **Hi-Tec Dirty Weekend** series, offer perfect stepping stones into multi-day adventure racing events.

INSET: Cargo nets and rope swings are challenges you may have to face in a sprint race.

clinics take place over a weekend in a suitably beautiful nature area and will see a group of experts
imparting their knowledge in disciplines varying from
the cerebral (strategy, orienteering, motivation,
nutrition and the like) to hands-on workshops focusing on how to handle your bike or abseil down a cliff.
These 'AR tasters' usually culminate in a 24-hour
race where you form a team and tramp off into the
dark to apply the skills you have learnt.

Further ways of buffing up your theory would be
to join AR discussion groups, chat rooms or Internet
forums, all of which offer handy hints to newcomers,
or 'newbies'. A more practical option may be to
offer your services as a volunteer race marshall or
backup-crew member to a team – a surefire way of
fast-tracking your multi-sport learning curve.

Once you decide to go all the way, test the AR
waters by sweating it out at one of the many sprint
races taking place in your area. Globally, the format
might differ in some respects, but basically you are
looking at an off-road triathlon, where you kick off
with an open-water swim or water leg (raft, kayak
or tube), then do a 20km (12-mile) or so cross-
country mountain-bike ride before finishing off
with a 5km (3-mile) trail run, sometimes including
a few surprise obstacles. Lasting anything from
two to four hours, these condensed outdoor
adventures pit teams against a course over a distance of about 30km (20 miles). Urban Challenges
put a slightly different spin on things, taking adventure racing out of the bush and into the concrete
jungle. Negotiating stairs on your bike, abseiling
down skyscrapers, crawling through pipes, pounding
pavements and dodging traffic suddenly become part
of the buzz. Distances might vary from a 25km (15-
mile) shortie to a day-long slog.

By now, you should be ready to pick up the pace
and face up to a short-course 'weekender'. Expect a
multi-day adventure race about 60–120km (37–75
miles) in distance, incorporating at least four disciplines and set within a spectacular natural environment. Mountain biking, trail running, trekking and

canyoneering (kloofing) could make up the mix, with
perhaps a paddle and an abseil thrown in for good
measure. Racing from dusk to dawn will be part of
the deal; the event can last for anything up to 32
hours – or more, if you decide to get horribly lost.
If you finish intact – and once you forget the pain
and the bugs and the disagreements about map
co-ordinates at four in the morning – you might
entertain visions of going all the way into the territory
of 'classic' adventure racing.

**ABOVE: The only gear required for a sprint race is a good pair of running shoes and the requisite
mountain-biking kit. However, a sturdy off-road bike, gloves and a helmet, clip-in shoes and a
hydration pack will help to improve your racing.**

Before you know it, you will be suckered into a desert challenge or lining up to toil for 10 never-ending days along a gruelling, rainforest stage race. These are ultra events where the dreaded sleep monster stalks the small hours, uniting with skull-crunching fatigue to test individual skills and team dynamics to the limit. Before you commit to ultra racing, remember this will require an obligation to long hours of training, a substantial investment in outdoor gear and the need to improve your skills level dramatically. Pushing the distance toward the 250km (150-mile) zone will see you stepping into

'classic' territory, racing for around 48 hours or more through multiple checkpoints and transitions. Go beyond this and you enter into true expedition racing, usually in an event where teams face an arduous, multi-day route, sometimes without the assistance of a backup or seconding crew. Athletes are expected to carry most of their own gear, food and supplies for 10 days or more, although the organizer may arrange a few gear drops along a course from 350–600km (220–375 miles) long.

Stage racing adds yet another variation to the AR concept, with racers aiming to complete individual legs

ABOVE: **Team dynamics really start coming into play during longer adventure races. Close teamwork, as displayed during a water crossing by Team Subaru of Canada, will contribute to a successful race.**

on consecutive days, then overnighting at predetermined rest areas before setting off on the next stage.

As Odyssey Adventure Racing's Don Mann puts it, 'A sprint race tests your body; a two-day race tests your mind; an expedition race tests your soul.'

These are your choices; now all you have to do is take a long and hard look at your personal physical condition and mental state and decide where and how to take your first step into AR.

Talking multi-sport

The more toys you get to play with, the more fun you can have! Think AR and you immediately think multiple disciplines, which means you can get stuck into anything from paddling or mountain biking to trekking and mountaineering in a single day. Proficiency in such a wide range of activities might initially seem a huge task, but your single biggest step will be just to do it. Begin by sticking to the basics – be well organized, properly equipped, concentrate on your navigation, do not push your body too hard and approach every separate stage as an individual mini-race. This will help you focus on the specific skills pertaining to that discipline and take your mind off the seemingly overwhelming task of stringing multiple activities together over an intimidating distance.

Key disciplines will be covered in more detail in Chapter Five (see pages 46–81), but let us assume you will start by doing a sprint race and can therefore focus on mountain biking, trail running and a water leg. The race sequence varies, depending on the race director or event, but often kicks off with an open-water swim of between 500m and 1km (¹/₂ mile). This may become a muddy or very wet mêlée, with people dunking each other in an effort to get to the front, so if you are not a water baby it would be best to hang back. Tube floats, rafting or flat-water canoeing might replace the swim, but basically the purpose of the water leg is to spread the field before the start of the next stage.

Depending on the racers' fitness, it will take approximately half an hour for the leaders to charge

RIGHT: **AR may involve disciplines as diverse as dog-sledding, desert mountain-biking or paddling an inflatable kayak through a fjord filled with icebergs.**

into a central transition area where a period of frenzied activity follows. Dump your wet gear (do not forget to clean your feet!), put on your mountain-bike top, hydration pack and helmet before cranking into a 20km (12-mile) off-road cycling route. With mountain biking generally making up 50 per cent of race time, this is where you could win or lose the battle. The route may vary from speedy and flat hard-pack to a sandy jeep track or, at a well-chosen venue, an exciting combination of challenging single-track, punishing climbs and white-knuckle downhills. A cycling computer will help you pace your race, a hydration pack is a must for hands-free drinking, while a lightweight hard-tail (with front suspension only) are essential.

An hour or more later, depending on terrain and fitness levels, you will be steaming into the transition area to gear up for the final assault. Swap your bike shoes for trail runners and hoof into the run, usually for about 5km (3 miles) and with a selection of mild to wild obstacles thrown in. On this stage you will be at the mercy of sadistic race directors, who might

set up anything from rope traverses and vertical nets to mud crawls and climbing walls. After two hours of high-intensity exercise, your legs will be jelly, your lungs pumping fire and you will wonder why you are doing this. Just when you think your heart might thump right through your rib cage, the finish line will heave into sight and you will realize that you have loved every gruelling, scintillating, mad second – and that you will do it all over again the first chance you get.

TOP: Water legs will let you make up precious time; if you can make it out of the water first, you can beat the rest of the bunch to the start of the next leg.
ABOVE: Team Maybe X-Din crosses the 2002 High Coast 400 finish line in first place.

Teaming up

By now you will have a reasonably good idea as to what AR is about and what to expect from the various disciplines during your first race. More decisions are in the pipeline, though: firstly, at what level will you be competing; and secondly, do you want to go solo or be a team player? There is no arguing that entering as an individual eliminates much of the pressure of organizing and interacting with additional team members, while racing as a pair enables you to team up comfortably with another athlete of similar skills and fitness levels – and obviously makes it easier to decide at what level to compete as you know each other's limitations. This and many other factors (terrain, temperature, fitness levels, gear and obstacles) will affect the time individual legs take, but a 25-minute swim, 75-minute bike and 30-minute run will probably see you finish in the top 20 per cent of the field.

Most sprint events are pitched at mixed teams of two to four (including at least one member of the opposite sex), as this comprehensively tests your team dynamics. With the exception of navigation, this rates as the one factor critical to successful racing, requiring members to communicate constantly and show relentless commitment during both preparation and the actual race.

Although teams usually appoint a captain, leadership responsibilities may shift during longer races, further compelling teams to devise strategies that take individual strengths and weaknesses into account. Essentially, your team will be as strong as its weakest member. Although a chauvinist perception persists of women as the weaker sex, there is no longer a gender gap in the sport of AR. In fact, women often demonstrate superior endurance and a knack for problem solving, especially during longer AR events (see 'Girl power' on page 87).

Do not think you are home and dry once you have put your team together; a successful move into multi-day racing without a motivated backup crew is unthinkable, and top teams will vigorously attest to this. Competitors recognize these unsung heroes of the AR fraternity as integral to the long tramp to victory and may take as much care in selecting seconds as they do when it comes to picking team members. No wonder, as seconds become nurses, chefs, masseuses, drivers, hurry-up-and-waiters, spiritual guides, mechanical whiz-kids and motivational gurus rolled into one, often acting as the glue keeping the unit together when the going gets tough. They must know team members intimately and cater to their every whim, pampering, feeding, dressing, counselling and berating them when they come into transition points. Bikes must be cleaned, potions mixed, boats readied and food prepared 24 hours a day – always with a smile and a few words of encouragement. Pick your seconds well and treat them like gold.

ABOVE: Trekking poles might not be necessary for sprint events, but will save your legs and knees over longer distances by redistributing up to 15 per cent of your body weight to your shoulders and arms. They also improve overall balance.

Finding your way

As we are touching on racing over longer distances, a quick overview on navigation will not go amiss. This critical AR component is often the defining factor in a successful race; the ability to orienteer your position on the ground relative to a map is essential. A pre-race briefing generally sees each team receiving a series of co-ordinates and maps. These are used by the team to plot a route incorporating compulsory control points – passport control points (PCs), transition points (TPs) or checkpoints (CPs) – along the route to ensure all teams complete the full course. An appointed team navigator takes responsibility for navigational matters and aids, such as a compass, maps, waterproof map case, protractor, distance roller and sharp pencil. It is vital, however, that someone acts as an understudy and can take over navigational duties should this become necessary.

Problem solving goes hand in hand with navigation and this is where race tactics and dynamics may make or break a team. Going in gung-ho will not win you any races, so keep your wits about you, conserve your energy and make 100 per cent sure of your navigation. Try to plan in such a way that you pass through difficult terrain in good light, get to bottle-necks at the front of the queue and have enough kick left at the end of the race to give it your best.

Taking the plunge

It is relatively expensive to gear up for AR, but you do not have to break the bank. Sprint event organizers realize they are dealing with a field filled with

TOP: **Navigation adds a cerebral component to adventure racing. If you are unsure of your position at any stage, always stop and consult your maps.**
ABOVE: **Ziploc™ bags or waterproof map cases will keep your maps dry.**

first timers and therefore supply most of the specialized equipment required. As you will be racing in a controlled environment, you can get by with the minimum of kit beyond your clothing, footwear, bicycle, helmet and backpack (see 'Core short-course kit items', page 34). Once you enter longer races, you will be faced with a dreaded 'Mandatory Equipment List' specific to each individual event. This lists compulsory items to be carried at all times; failure to comply with the regulations could lead either to disqualification or the imposition of hefty time penalties. Expect to carry a dry set of clothing, maps and navigational equipment, a sleeping bag or shelter, survival blanket, torch, whistle, pencil flare, multi-tool, plus enough

water and food to last you at least 24 hours. A basic first-aid kit per team is non-negotiable. Remember that this list indicates the minimum equipment needed to compete, so check with the race director or other racers about any items that may prove handy along a certain course.

Best is to be prepared, so visualize every discipline from start to finish or, even better, do a dummy race and plan accordingly. Kit lists are issued even for shorter races, so make sure you are au fait with gear essentials for the various disciplines. No certification is required, although organizers will expect you to sign a basic disclaimer before the race. If it makes you more comfortable, sign up for a skills clinic or racing academy to boost your confidence in disciplines you feel unsure about. These classes are often presented in conjunction with short-course events, or you could check AR resources on the Internet for courses presented in your area. From a training point of view, you will have to push yourself both aerobically and technically, opting to spend equal amounts of time on your feet and on your bike. Paddling, open-water swimming and focused muscle-building sessions must be part of the mix, as must at least one 12-hour, non-stop practice race per month.

So why do it? Adventure racers admit they stop counting after a while how many times they are asked this question. Every individual has a different answer anyway; some do it to conquer personal demons, others to worship at the altar of the great outdoors, many are addicted to the opium of achieving the seemingly impossible, while a good few are unsure of the answer themselves. Whatever your reason, adventure racing compels you to step beyond your physical, mental and spiritual comfort zones into uncharted territory, enabling you to look at yourself and the world in a fresh and unfettered way. The camaraderie, courage, ecstasy and agony that shine through during an adventure race are probably as real as life gets. For those who triumph over the gruelling terrain and gut-thumping fatigue, there is the holy grail of spiritual and mental regeneration.

ABOVE: A lightweight mountain-bike will not only be easier for you to pedal uphill, but will also make your life easier when you have to carry your bike across terrain that is impossible to cycle. Some racers may opt for cycle-cross bikes.

Thinking through the race

'EXPECT THINGS TO GO WRONG' might as well be the first rule of adventure racing. No matter how well you plan or how much time you put into contingencies, at some stage something is bound to go awry. But do not worry; a seemingly insurmountable setback, especially during longer races lasting a week or more, may seem no more than a temporary glitch by the time you get to day six. It is imperative to focus first on dealing with the problem as efficiently as possible and then set up systems to ensure it does not happen again. Damage control is the key and this chapter will go some way toward helping you to limit the chaos, as well as to ensure that you finish what you start.

Forewarned is forearmed

The best way of dealing with the unpredictable nature of adventure racing is to be fully aware of what could go wrong, so ensure you are as informed as possible. This means researching every aspect of the race, from the vegetation in the region where you will be racing and expected seasonal weather conditions, to probable route options linked to local adventure

Researching the race:

RACE INFORMATION
Read race reports concerning previous races conducted by the race director; all directors tend to set similar problems. Speak to previous competitors. Check reconnaissance reports/videos produced for the media for insight into major features of the race.

MAPS
Source maps of the area and get used to the scale and symbols. Use aeronautical maps for remote areas.

LOCAL RESOURCES
A team member should reach the race area earlier to find out where food and outdoor equipment may be obtained.

INTERNET
This is a valuable tool to find information about the country and weather.

ESSENTIAL QUESTIONS
1. Where will the race take place, nearest airport, station, etc.?
2. How will you travel from the airport to race registration?
3. Do you need a support vehicle?
4. Are there any restrictions regarding size of bike and/or equipment boxes?
5. Can you ship items in advance?
6. What type of weather can be expected during the race?
7. Is water safe to drink (gardia) and swim in (bilharzia)?
8. Is local wildlife dangerous?
9. What medical precautions are recommended, e.g. malaria, rabies.
10. Do you need to hire equipment such as sea kayaks?
11. What level of training/certification is required for each discipline?
12. What equipment is prohibited? Get clarification from the race director.
13. Have you all the items on the kit list?

David Ogden, Team International Adventurers

TOP: **Involve the team as a whole in researching the race, thus ensuring a minimum of surprises at the pre-race briefing.**
INSET: **Ensure your equipment, especially your bike, is properly serviced before the race.**

activities. The longitude, latitude and altitude of your race destination give a broad idea of vegetation, topography and terrain, but you would do better to speak to a local who knows the area or to fellow athletes who have previously raced there.

Annual weather specifics (such as average temperatures and seasonal rainfall figures) add to the databank you are compiling on a specific area, but are generalized. To predict local weather conditions, access a medium-term weather forecast for the region you will be racing in, taking note of extreme phenomena predicted for the race duration. Ascertain conditions, especially rainfall, in the area for the week before your arrival: heavy downpours may indicate swollen rivers or muddy roads, influencing your gear selection when it comes to paddling craft, mountain bikes and footwear. Also, learn the tides, currents, water depths, sunset, moon rise and moon set.

Detailed topographical maps of a region are a veritable fount of factual information, enabling you not only to check the topography and vegetation, but also to study rivers, mountain ranges, canyons and other geographical features that might be included in the individual race stages. Ask regional tourism authorities to send you all brochures relevant to local outdoor adventure activities – race directors are suckers for outstanding areas of natural beauty and will invariably include thundering waterfalls, whitewater rapids and high-altitude trekking trails in their race plans. Take into consideration the predicted discipline distances (sometimes released before the event), the number of days the race will last, and any previous races in this area. Use your head, start doing your sums and, with a bit of luck, you could string together a reasonable idea of what to expect when race day dawns.

Lastly, and very importantly, involve your backup crew in the research process, or at least distribute briefing notes to ensure everyone is fully aware of any information relevant to your race strategy.

ABOVE: **Vegetation will influence your on-the-ground route choices. Here competitors stick to a dirt road during Adventure Quest Africa in order to avoid having to bash their way through the thorny bush on either side.**

Motivating mind and body

The age-old dictum that success is one per cent inspiration and 99 per cent perspiration could easily have been coined specifically for adventure racing. It might seem a simplistic view, but if you put in the requisite time – both physically and mentally – you are bound to reap the rewards. Now that you have done your research regarding the race, the next step is to focus on preparing your mind and body for what lies ahead.

Due to the unpredictability of AR, you might find your physical build-up easier to cope with than the corresponding mental preparation. At least you will have a basic idea of which disciplines will make up the race and the approximate distances, and can prepare accordingly. Ideally, you would therefore be able to plan your training programme to simulate these expected activities and distances, thus priming your body to cope on the day of the race.

The environment you train in will further affect your physical preparedness, so try to get your body used to comparative terrain, humidity, temperature and gear; this will boost your performance once you go into race mode. In a nutshell, do not train on level ground if the race is set in the Rockies; get used to the suck of sand if you will be trekking through desert dunes; and do your running with the pack weight you are expecting to carry during the actual race. This will help you ascertain your level of fitness, as well as assist you in calculating your true speed of advance in the various disciplines with more confidence.

ABOVE: **Your training sessions should be set in conditions similar to those where you will be racing, so to get ready for Namibia's Desert Challenge you would practise trekking through thick sand in high temperatures.**

An effective training programme will gradually boost your endurance level by building your cardiovascular fitness, then focus on strengthening specific muscle groups, and finally allow you to concentrate on specific skills, so you can maximize your competence in mountain biking, paddling, mountaineering and other disciplines.

Your physical build-up must be carefully managed and must recognize wider issues such as nutrition and team interaction. It is of no value if you can personally maintain a speed of advance of 7min/km while the rest of the team is lagging two minutes behind. This is why training together is so important; it teaches you to recognize each other's strengths and weaknesses, and compels you to communicate. Do not internalize issues; rather be open with team members, allowing the unit as a whole to deal with issues before they become problems. After all, crossing the finish line in first place without your teammates counts for nothing.

When it comes to nutrition, plan your training meals and snacks to correspond with foodstuff available during the actual race if possible. Sojourns into exotic locations may make this difficult, but you can at least make sure you race on supplements and snacks to which everyone in the team responds positively. You are in this together, so help each other to finish it together.

Which brings us to matters of the mind. While physical exercise is a concrete activity – you run, you sweat, your muscles ache and you come back having achieved a specific goal – mental preparation is a journey into a realm of intangibles. It is in the mind that self-belief, motivation and determination do battle with conflict, panic and fear of the unknown. This is where your race will be won or lost. The benefits of sports psychology have been proven beyond doubt in recent years, and most endurance athletes now per-

ceive it as imperative to their training. But motivational strategies are as diverse and plentiful as the multitude of physical training programmes, so adopt an approach suited to you and your team. Areas to address include goal setting, accepting the unpredictable nature of the sport, clarifying individual roles and responsibilities within the group, determining decision-making mechanisms, and foreseeing various scenarios. Try to visualize the race in your mind before setting off, thinking through the various stages while mentally dealing with possible obstacles. This positive affirmation, or autosuggestion, will subconsciously prime your mind and help you to solve problems effectively if and when they occur.

TOP: **Controlled skills training, such as practising eskimo rolls in a swimming pool, will boost your confidence when things go wrong on the water during the race.**
ABOVE: **Always wear protective headgear when shooting whitewater rapids, as you never know whether you might capsize.**

A host of compounding factors will gnaw at your psyche, including fatigue, dehydration and pain. Sleep deprivation will probably be one of the main mental strains you will face during the race, but is not something you can train for physiologically. You can, however, prepare yourself mentally to cope with minimal sleep (see box below). Two hours a night is a proven remedy; AR guru Don Mann recommends sleeping at 04:00 and letting the sun and your natural sleep cycle wake you at about 06:00. He also cautions against sleeping in check-points, which are too comfortable and may tempt you to stay too long.

Coping with sleep deprivation

1. You cannot 'bank' sleep before an event but you can ensure you are well rested. Getting eight to nine hours of sleep a night for at least two weeks before a race makes a difference.

2. During prolonged exercise, carbohydrates can delay the onset of fatigue. For best performance, eat low Glycaemic Index (GI) carbohydrates (e.g. chickpeas, yoghurt, apples, soybeans, barley, lentils), which are broken down slowly, releasing glucose into the blood for an extended period (see page 117).

3. If you keep alert and motivated through mental stimulation, one or two nights' loss of sleep should not significantly impair your physical performance. Assign specific tasks to each team member, such as navigation, distance judgment, altitude confirmation, landmark and attack point identification.

4. Plan your sleep strategy to allow for short power naps and longer sleep sessions. Delaying sleep until you can barely keep your eyes open will completely exhaust your body, minimizing the effectiveness of short naps when you finally give in.

5. Preferably avoid 'stay-awake' medications. Prolonged activity, little sleep and extreme conditions all make your body react differently to drugs and may result in adverse and possibly even life-threatening conditions.

Lisa de Speville

TOP AND ABOVE: Early morning race starts and racing through the night (top) are likely to put you on the back foot, but a 15-minute catnap (above) will go a long way to refreshing both your mind and body.

Developing team synergy

The main challenge faced by most teams is simply being a team. These tips for maintaining harmony will give you the best chance of developing that highly elusive ingredient – synergy.

1. Agree on your goals. Having one person gunning for the win while another simply wants to finish creates unwelcome divisions in the team.

2. Communicate openly and honestly. Avoid hiding feelings or bottling up annoyances, which can easily percolate into an irresolvable conflict. Raise issues with sensitivity and without acrimony.

3. Address any conflict that does arise quickly and effectively to avoid spending valuable energy arguing rather than moving forward.

4. See challenges, not problems. See adventure racing as an endless series of necessary challenges requiring agility and flexibility to overcome. Make mistakes a learning opportunity. Mistakes can be costly, but learning from them gives you the experience not to make them again.

5. Offer and accept help. Everyone on the team will be both the strongest and the weakest athlete at some point during a long race. To keep the team moving at optimal speed, everyone needs to share his or her load and push, pull and carry. Ask for help and accept it whenever necessary.

6. Learn to trust and respect your teammates. Trust that all are working toward the common goal (see 1 above) and treat each team member with respect. In return, you will be trusted and respected – something that helps to build valuable friendships and a strong team.

Ian Adamson, Team Nike ACG / Balance Bar

ABOVE: Ian Adamson and his teammates from Team Nike ACG/Balance Bar know the importance of functioning synergistically, communicating openly to resolve potential problems and helping to keep each other motivated and focused.

Survival tips when things go wrong

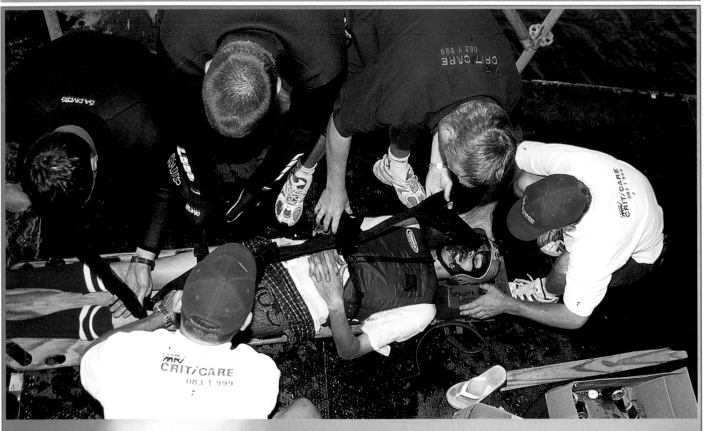

1. Dress and pack for the worst possible weather conditions you could expect along the route.

2. When things go wrong, do not panic. Stop, think and discuss the options with your teammates.

3. Never race without basic survival items such as a whistle, waterproof matches, knife, length of rope, survival blanket, compass, torch and pencil flare.

4. Carry an up-to-date, approved first-aid kit and ensure at least two team members have completed a relevant first-aid course.

5. Ascertain beforehand if anyone in the team suffers from a condition requiring special medication or care.

6. Use your whistle, flare or any other means of signalling to attract attention if you can hear a search party looking for you.

7. Always pack an extra set of clothes – being dry is the first step to keeping warm.

8. If you find that you feel disoriented at night, get some sleep and rethink your situation in daylight.

9. Once you can see, move to high ground and try to orient yourself on your map.

10 Carry enough water and emergency food rations to last you 24–48 hours.

ABOVE: Although every team must always carry a basic first-aid kit, it is imperative for race organizers to ensure that they have professional medical personnel on stand-by in case of emergencies.

Making it safe

AR is a sport fraught with possible dangers, yet for many racers this constitutes the very essence of its attraction. But as in any other sporting code, both race organizers and competitors must adhere to certain safety standards. Until recently, racers were prepared to accept the excuse, 'This is AR, what do you expect?' when things went wrong, but in an age where professionalism, sponsorship and prize money have become part of the game, this is no longer acceptable. Codes of Conduct have been adopted by the sport's governing bodies in most countries where AR is practised, effectively compelling race organizers and participants to subscribe to a basic set of rules and regulations. Credible race directors have also created systems to assure a reasonable level of safety, with certification concerning technically demanding disciplines, such as mountaineering and whitewater paddling, fast becoming the rule.

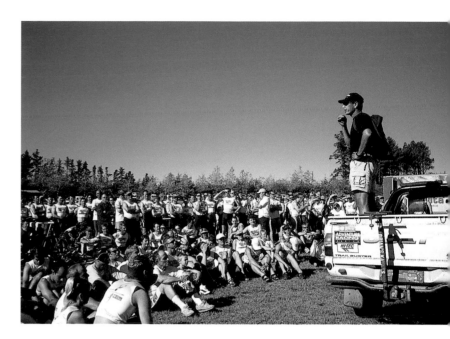

These days, most major events incorporate at least one day of acclimatization and competency testing before the race starts. Experts in a variety of outdoor disciplines put competitors through their paces to ensure they have the skills to cope with compulsory activities along the route. These practical sessions cover anything from setting up a belay (safety anchor) while abseiling, to doing an Eskimo roll while kayaking, or performing a self-arrest with an ice axe. Certificates of competency by internationally ratified accreditation organizations might also be a condition of race entry. (One thing both racers and organizers should keep in mind is that the ability to perform a skill within a controlled environment demonstrates only basic competence; the true test comes after 72 hours without sleep, shrouded in total darkness and in sub-zero temperatures.)

There is always an implied expectation that AR competitors are adept at coping with life-threatening situations. Anything can – and regularly does – happen along the route, from getting lost for 48 hours, to breaking an ankle or close encounters with venomous snakes. As a racer, you must be confident that you have the skills and temperament to deal with such situations; teaching you all the necessary survival techniques is beyond the scope of this handbook. The key to staying alive is to plan correctly, race within your ability, pack the requisite items to shelter you from the elements, and have enough food and water to see you through an emergency.

While race organizers are required to have the necessary infrastructure in place to launch search and rescue operations at the drop of a hat, there is no guarantee they will make it to you in time. Pay attention to the pre-race safety briefing, ensuring you know what steps to take in case of a medical or other emergency. Identify possible risks along your route and actively plan preventive strategies; carry ample water to prevent dehydration, wear a hat and sunscreen to avoid sunstroke, and take no unnecessary chances. Use your flares only in an emergency, stick together as a team if possible or, if one of you is incapacitated, send someone to the nearest checkpoint or transition for help. Chances are things will go wrong, so make sure you know how to cope with the situation by reading 'Survival tips when things go wrong' on page 30.

ABOVE: **Listen carefully during the pre-race briefing and, if you have any doubt regarding emergency procedures, make sure that you ask your questions while you have a chance rather than when it is too late.**

Race safety: the race organizer's responsibilities

COMMUNICATIONS AND MONITORING

A competent race headquarters and communications centre are mandatory so you can access any information at any time. Good backup systems are vital. VHF radios, mobile and satellite phones should supplement each other, with more than one system at remote checkpoints. Assign specific responsibilities to officials who know the local conditions.

MARSHALLING

Officials at checkpoints must have a basic knowledge of first aid, how to recognize and treat fatigue, dehydration, hypo-/hyperthermia, hypoglycemia, bruises, cuts and fractures. Give them a handbook telling them what to do in case of an accident.

TRANSPORTATION

Have a plan for evacuating a racer from any point along the route. Be able to keep a cool head and improvise when the unexpected happens. Although racers demand challenges, surprises and a sense of risk, they expect organizers to cope with any emergency and maintain the highest possible level of safety.

KNOW YOUR ROUTE

Spectators, sponsors and the media want excitement and some degree of danger. Know the area well, visiting all route sections before the race so you are aware of inherent ·dangers (rockfalls, glaciers, streams, weather patterns, danger areas). Plan the race to accommodate last-minute route changes if conditions change, presenting unacceptable levels of danger.

KNOW AND INFORM THE RACERS

Clarify to the teams exactly what they are taking on; incompetent teams should not be allowed to race. Inform racers of special conditions that might arise and keep in mind that they might choose a dangerous route if they are not clearly discouraged from doing so.

EQUIPMENT, GEAR AND SKILLS CHECKS

Compile a comprehensive equipment list, with safety as a primary parameter. Do not take gear and skills checks lightly. For a multi-stage race, carry out gear checks before each stage. Only competent officials should be responsible for gear checks. Give teams failing skills tests ample time to acquire the skills under the guidance of a competent instructor.

Hans Christian Florian, co-race director, Arctic Team Challenge

ABOVE: **Race marshalls who are monitoring mountaineering and other technical race sections should have the requisite skills in order to guide racers proficiently through the specific stage they are monitoring.**

Racing green

Respect for the environment is one of the fundamental tenets of adventure racing. With events regularly taking place in some of our planet's most pristine ecological zones, it is a non-negotiable principle. Constant awareness of the consequence of your actions along the route is necessary; no matter how exhausted or sleep deprived you are, stick to the rules of minimum impact.

Often, damage is done without someone realizing it, so take it upon yourself to educate fellow athletes regarding environmental issues. Like hiking, AR is moving more and more toward the principle of 'packing out what you pack in'. Within exceptionally fragile ecosystems, this includes human waste and tampons. In less sensitive zones, you may get away with digging a trench of about 15–20cm (6–8in) deep and, where possible, using stove fuel to burn the toilet paper and other offending material. Other waste, including all paper, plastic, tin foil and foreign matter, should be packed out to your seconding crew or to the next transition. Use biodegradable soap when washing or doing the dishes, and do so away from any water source to avoid the risk of contamination.

When moving along a designated trail, stick to the route instead of taking shortcuts that may later cause erosion. Some race directors file special-use permits that do not cover deviations from the intended course. Do not damage the vegetation by cutting walking sticks or breaking branches to mark your trail. Try to avoid confrontation with the local fauna for both your sake and theirs, remembering that even the smallest creatures may pack an unexpected punch while protecting their home.

The ethos of racing green extends beyond simply being environmentally aware while you are on the trail. When you are buying your equipment, look for companies that utilize recycled material during manufacture, opt for environmentally friendly packaging, and try to buy brands supported by a non-exploitative labour policy.

Very importantly, if you are racing through an inhabited area, remember your manners when you come into contact with the indigenous inhabitants. Be polite and courteous at all times and, above all, find out about the local customs and respect them. Never forget that racing within these unspoilt areas of natural beauty is a privilege – not a right.

ABOVE: **Respect for the environment and for the local inhabitants of the region in which the race is being held is non-negotiable. This includes not damaging crops or flaunting local customs. Always follow the rules of minimum impact.**

Kit inspection

NOBODY EVER SAID this was going to be an inexpensive exercise, but rest assured, there are ways of kitting yourself out for adventure racing without breaking the bank.

First decide at what level you will be racing and buy your kit accordingly: if your aim is to start with sprint races, stick to basic items and add to your gear as and when you move up to the next level. Keep costs down by trying before you buy. Your personal body geometry, shape and size are unique and you need to try out items – especially packs, footwear and bikes – to find models, sizes and configurations to which your body responds positively.

Many stores now offer indoor testing areas, allowing you to get to grips with the feel and quality of an item before buying. Get input from fellow racers, follow gear discussions on online AR chat rooms and read gear-test columns in magazines and on websites. Set yourself a realistic budget, draw up a shopping list and then head for the shops, comparing price, payment terms, features, guarantees or warranties, and after-sales service. If you know exactly what you want, shop on-line and enjoy the convenience of having the product delivered to your front door.

Core AR clothing:

Check that you and your team are wearing the following items before you set off on the various disciplines:

1   **On foot:**
    trail shoes, seamless socks, non-chafe shorts or thermal longs, wicking top, protective shell, thermal fleece, peak cap ✓

2   **On your bike:**
    clip-in mountain-biking shoes, tight socks, fleece top, padded shorts, breathable top, protective shell, helmet, eyewear, gloves ✓

3   **On the water:**
    aqua booties, paddling shorts or wetsuit, thermal top, paddling jacket, paddling helmet (for whitewater) ✓

Gearing up for the race

Various factors will influence your purchasing decision, not the least of which will be your budget. Be realistic; if you are an average racer into AR for the fun of it, there is no need to blow your bank balance on the latest full-suspension bike or hi-tech pack. But do buy the best you can afford, as there is no point

TOP: A team is gear-checked by officials before the start of the 2003 Arctic Team Challenge.
INSET: Always secure items such as compasses and whistles with a lanyard to avoid the chance of losing them.

in wasting money on poorly manufactured gear likely to fall apart before the end of your first race.

Also ascertain which gear items will be supplied by the organizers at the races you intend doing during the year. It does not make sense to blow your budget on items you might only use once or twice a year, especially if these are supplied free of charge or available for hire at a reasonable rate.

Another important consideration is the environment in which you will be racing; as a rule of thumb, the more extreme the environment, the more you will need to depend on your gear and the higher the price you can expect to pay. Imagine sub-zero tundras, alpine peaks and Grade 5 whitewater rapids and you will immediately understand that these are situations where you must be able to trust your kit absolutely to keep you safe.

Seeing that we have already looked at basic gear requirements for a sprint race in Chapter Two (see page 17), it makes sense now to consider some additional items you need during longer races. Always check the Mandatory Equipment List to make sure you comply with the range of gear prescribed by the race organizers; fail to do so and you might be disqualified or incur a time penalty.

AR gear checklist

Gear needs vary from race to race depending on the required disciplines, but the following kit list for the two-day Endorphin Fix event organized by Odyssey Adventure Racing (courtesy of *The Complete Guide to Adventure Racing* by Don Mann and Kara Schaad) gives a good idea of what you might need during an unsupported 200km (125-mile) event.

PERSONAL GEAR
Biking: mountain bike; approved bike helmets; lights attached to bike – white front, red rear, battery life for 14 hours; repair kit (spare tubes, patches); pump. Clipless shoes may be staged with the bike. Recommended: bike gloves, map case, rear bike rack.

Boating: personal kayak paddles may be used, but must be carried the entire race; Coast Guard approved life jacket (minimum Type III – no inflatable life jackets acceptable); helmet (bike or climbing helmet is acceptable); commercial grade throw bag (with minimum 15m/50ft of rope), one per boat; dry-bag or waterproof container (garbage bags not acceptable); knife and whistle within easy reach while on water. Skill certificate required for every competitor.

Climbing: climbing harness; three locking carabiners (Figure 8 or ATC – no other devices acceptable); climbing-specific helmet, with lights after 19:00 (no bike or boating helmet allowed on climb); sling or daisy chain if you will hang your pack during the descent. Skill certificate required for every competitor; you must be checked off with the gear you will be racing with.

TEAM/SOLO MEDICAL KIT band-aids; gauze; adhesive/duct tape; iodine/alcohol swabs; analgesic; iodine tablets or purifier for water purification – reasonable amounts for a two-day race.

MANDATORY GEAR to be carried throughout the competition by each racer: lighter; knife with minimum 6cm (2.5in) blade (folding is acceptable); whistle; head lamp/batteries; fleece-type top; Gore-Tex-type shell; land compass (one per every two competitors). GPS not allowed.

ODYSSEY PROVIDES clue book and course directions; boats and paddles; ropes set-up; maps of the course; communications; medical support; manned checkpoints; prizes and awards; pre- and post-race food.

Don Mann, Odyssey Adventure Racing

ABOVE: Make sure that all of your personal gear has been packed into clearly marked or colour-coded crates before the start of the race. This helps to prevent confusion and save time later, when speed is of the essence.

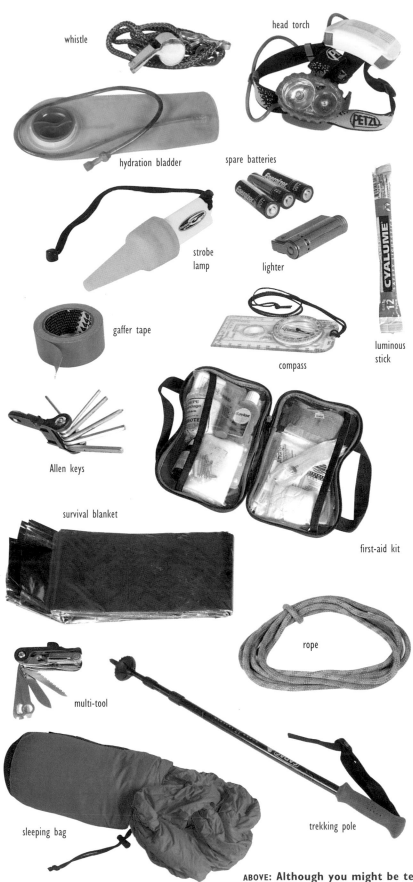

whistle

head torch

hydration bladder

spare batteries

strobe lamp

lighter

luminous stick

gaffer tape

compass

Allen keys

first-aid kit

survival blanket

rope

multi-tool

sleeping bag

trekking pole

Check your person and pack the following: hydration bladder and/or bottles, head torch with sufficient spare batteries, bike, helmet, spare tyres and gloves, the compulsory whistle, survival blanket, lighter and knife or multi-tool. Appropriate clothing (covered in more detail opposite), as well as food and water supplies sufficient for at least 24 hours, are also part of the deal. In addition, the team as a whole needs to carry at least two sleeping bags, a compass (preferably two), first-aid kit, tent bivvy or appropriate shelter, 10m (33ft) safety rope, bicycle pump, tool kit, pencil/smoke flare, Lumi-Stick or strobe lamp. Lastly, pack any certificates of competency relevant to technical stages making up part of the race. (See 'AR gear check list' on page 35.)

Organizers usually supply most of the gear required during specialized disciplines, but it is critical to confirm specifics with them well in advance. Kit items could include anything from water-specific gear, such as boats, personal flotation devices (PFDs), paddles, spray skirts and throw bags, to mountaineering equipment, such as dynamic ropes, friction or ascender devices, harnesses and helmets. Double-check your requirements with hire companies, ensuring they supply you with boats, paddles and other gear anatomically suited to you and the rest of the team. One final tip: test everything before the actual race.

Dress sense

Clothing is an integral part of your kit and any journey into AR territory will necessitate technical garments of the highest quality. Many prodigious advances in outdoor clothing technology have been driven by the needs of athletes pushing themselves and their gear to the limits within extreme situations, thus initiating the birth of a range of so-called miracle fibres. These advanced 'technical' fibres (including internationally registered brands such as Gore-Tex™, Pertex™, Tactel™ and the Polartec™ family of products) make for multi-functional adventure garments with a range of performance characteristics to enable you to cope with extreme

ABOVE: Although you might be tempted to try to make do with the minimum required kit, recognize that items such as first-aid kits, torches, safety ropes and compasses are non-negotiable. Remember that cold weather shortens battery life.

conditions without compromising on weight, breathability, insulation or durability. Fabrics to choose from include nylon (affordable, hard-wearing and light), polyester (relatively expensive, but quick-drying and very light) and various synthetic fibre blends aimed at improving the overall properties of the garment. GoLite™, a universal leader in outdoor clothing and gear, maximizes moisture management through the use of hollow-core and open-channel, C-shaped fibres, enabling garments to channel perspiration away from the skin and increase the area – and thus speed – of dissipation.

All around the globe, other major brands use proprietary technology to manufacture more effective outdoor clothing, creating lighter, warmer technical garments for everyone from sprint event amateurs to expedition race professionals. Although natural fibres like wool and mohair are staging a spirited comeback (think Smartwool socks), they are generally quite bulky so manufacturers tend to combine them with synthetic fibres. Steer clear of cotton, though – it absorbs way too much water and therefore offers little protection when you are wet and cold.

Make layering your religion when dressing for adventure racing; this is the most effective way of protecting yourself against the elements. Slip into a close-fitting base layer that will wick moisture away from the skin and speed up evaporation, thus keeping your body dry and allowing it to breathe unimpeded. In cold weather, you might choose a thermal base layer to help trap body heat. Next is a thermodynamic mid-layer, constructed to allow maximum comfort, heat retention and freedom of movement, as well as to control your body temperature without adding too much bulk or weight. The final layer is a hard-wearing,

waterproof Sealskinz™ socks

warm waterproof gloves

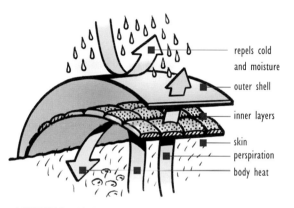

repels cold and moisture
outer shell
inner layers
skin
perspiration
body heat

LAYERING: MOISTURE AND HEAT MANAGEMENT

Buff™

ABOVE: The layering principle demonstrated by Michelle Lombardi of Team Mazda/First Ascent helps regulate body temperature during the race. Additional items such as waterproof socks, gloves and scarves are essential components of your body armour.

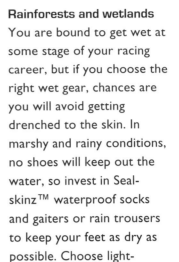

windproof and waterproof outer shell, usually consisting of garments aimed at protecting you from wind, rain and snow. Since much of your heat is lost through your head, and extremities like hands and feet are extremely susceptible to cold, items such as protective gloves, thermal socks, beanies, Buffs and scarves make up the remainder of your body armour.

Your clothing must cope with the extremities you will encounter within a specific race region, so dress with the expected ecosystems in mind. Below is a list of clothing items and considerations to think about when taking on extreme environments.

Deserts

Sky-high temperatures and the full glare of the sun necessitate quick-drying, well-ventilated garments with highly breathable fabrics to regulate your core temperature effectively. Protect your skin from ultraviolet (UV) damage and avoid dehydration by covering up with loose-fitting, long-sleeved shirts and long trousers (some manufacturers now incorporate a UV shield in their fabrics). Wear a wide-brimmed hat or flap-cap, and slather on the sunscreen. Also opt for light colours to ensure your garment reflects rather than absorbs the sun's rays. Eye protection is a must; choose polarizing lenses to reflect UV glare and guard against dust and sand. Keep in mind that night-time temperatures in the desert often dip below zero degrees, necessitating a thermal base as well as a mid-layer to keep warm.

Rainforests and wetlands

You are bound to get wet at some stage of your racing career, but if you choose the right wet gear, chances are you will avoid getting drenched to the skin. In marshy and rainy conditions, no shoes will keep out the water, so invest in Seal-skinz™ waterproof socks and gaiters or rain trousers to keep your feet as dry as possible. Choose light-coloured fabrics to help you spot leeches or other nasties, and wear mosquito netting around your hat to foil flying bug attacks. Wear a poncho or waterproof shell with a reticulated hood and stiff peak to keep rain out of your face and your upper body dry. Always carry a spare base layer and at least two pairs of dry socks, and stop to change these regularly to keep your feet in good condition. Treat your garments with Nikwax™ or a similar polymer coating to improve water repellency and use garbage bags and rain covers to keep the contents of your pack dry.

Sub-zero environments

Here we are talking about the Big Freeze – Arctic tundras, alpine peaks or any other frigid environment guaranteed to tax your clothing to the limit. Thermal layering is the way to go as layering will trap air, and therefore heat, to maintain your core temperature. A fleece mid-layer, insulated trousers, thermal socks, neck scarves and balaclavas or beanies will shield you from the cold, while a technical, hooded jacket, waterproof boots and gaiters or over-trousers will keep out the snow, wind and rain. Wraparound sunglasses with extreme glare protection are useful in helping you to cope with harsh reflections from the snow.

ABOVE LEFT: Always dress for your environment, choosing clothes that protect you without impeding your movement. Layering works in the desert, rainforest or snow.
TOP RIGHT: In wet terrain, wear quick-drying, water-shedding clothes and shoes.

Gearing up: the basics

Use this list of core clothing items as a starting point and add to it if you venture into more extreme environments.

FEET

- Light and sturdy trail shoes (boots may be preferred in extreme environments)

  trail shoe

- Clipless mountain biking shoes with padded tongue, recessed cleats, rigid toe cage and shock-absorbing rand (rubber strip around footbed)
- Several pairs of breathable socks (preferably also a waterproof pair or two)

LEGS:

- Lightweight, quick-drying shorts with drawstring and inner mesh lining
- Cycling-specific shorts (or padded inners worn underneath your racing shorts)

  padded shorts

- Thermal or lycra leggings in colder climates (or leg warmers)
- Underwear: many racers do without, but you do get gender-specific, breathable undies
- Waterproof over-trousers for extreme, wet-weather situations
- Gaiters to keep water and debris out of your shoes/socks and to protect your legs against scratching

  waterproof over-trousers

TORSO:

- Lightweight, quick-drying, breathable, moisture-wicking, long-sleeve and short-sleeve base-layer shirts
- Thermal, long-sleeve base-layer garment for cold and/or wet weather
- Mid-layer fleece with dynamic stretch when added thermal protection is needed
- Lightweight, windproof, water-resistant, breathable outer shell for mild racing environments
- Waterproof, insulated jacket with hood, tape-sealed seams, draw cords, venting, zipped pockets and drop-tail back design for more extreme situations

thermodynamic top

wrist-top computer

OTHER

- *Headwear*
  caps with drop-down neck flaps and breathing panels for summer; balaclavas, thermal beanies, neck scarves, ear warmers and Buffs™ for winter
- *Gloves*
  a dedicated selection including cycling, waterproof and insulated thermal options
- *Eyewear*
  polarized sunglasses to protect against UV rays, dust, snow and sleet
- *Watch*
  wrist-top computer with electronic compass, barometer, stopwatch and altimeter

protective eyewear

waterproof shell jacket

ABOVE: **More than anything else, your clothes — especially your shoes — should fit you well. Always test new gear during pre-race training sessions to ascertain its suitability for the even tougher race conditions.**

clip-in mountain-bike shoe

old trail runner needing
replacement

AR shoe

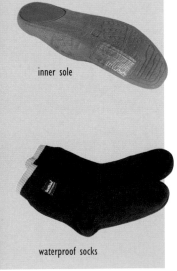

inner sole

waterproof socks

Footwear facts

Get this into your head: when your feet give in, your race is over. And since you can expect to spend up to half the race on your feet, your footwear should be selected with care. Put your foot down and try before you buy. Make sure the shoes you select fit well, suit the shape of your feet, and correct physiological problem areas such as pronation (ankles rolling inward). Carpeting does not count as AR terrain, so take the shoes outside and bounce on gravel, roots or bricks to get an idea of the cushioning and sole protection. (Best bring your pack; it is scary how much difference an extra 10–12kg (22–26lb) can make to the characteristics of shoes.) Most adventure racers opt for rugged, off-road trail-running shoes – preferably a model with breathable panels that expel water efficiently – with effective forefoot support, snug ankle fit (to avoid debris), hard-wearing sole with ample cushioning, sturdy heel counter to absorb impact, an aggressive tread pattern, and a cinch (quick-lock) lacing system. As a rule, AR shoes embrace many key characteristics of a good approach shoe (lightweight walking shoe), supplying greater foot support and more cushioning on long endurance treks. Trail terrain, climate and temperature will undoubtedly influence your shoe choices – you would not head into sub-zero alpine peaks wearing flimsy trail runners. In such situations, the environment might dictate an upgrade to boots, preferably of the waterproof, technical variety with minimal seaming, additional insulation and effortless compatibility with crampons. Part and parcel of the footwear issue is the need for good socks, so do not expect to get away with common or garden variety tennis socks. Avoid thick socks, which tend to bunch and retain moisture – both leading causes of blistering. Many top AR athletes swear by Sealskinz™, waterproof, neoprene socks that come in a choice of mid-calf or knee-length. They breathe well, but if you wear them in wet weather without rain trousers or gaiters, may actually collect water and leave you sloshing about. Dual-layered socks also work well, and brands such as Thousand Mile™ offer a durable, woven outer layer and a Tactel™ inner sleeve, thus assisting in moisture control while minimizing friction and effectively eliminating chafing and blisters.

Trail shoe design

1. Water-resistant mesh upper
2. Loops for fast and secure lacing
3. Gusset tongue to keep debris out
4. Comfortable padded tongue and collar
5. Heel tab to aid fitting and removal
6. Moulded overlay for protective fit
7. Grooves to bend shoe with movement
8. Midsole provides maximum cushioning
9. Extra strengthening to provide maximum control
10. Shock absorbing extra cushion pads
11. Grooves for forefoot flexibility
12. Outer sole traction for grip and stability
13. Heel pad to provide cushioning from impact

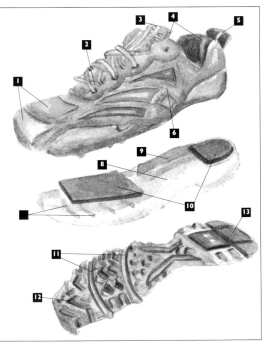

ABOVE LEFT: **Invest in the right footwear, replacing trail runners when they show signs of wear. AR shoes are sturdier than ordinary trail runners to cope with longer distances and greater pack weight. Inner soles with corrective pads do wonders for posture problems.**

10 foot-care tips

1. Never race in new shoes. Shoes need time to conform to the shape of your feet; wear them in over a number of shorter events. Consider orthopaedic insoles to reduce foot/back pain.

2. Keep your feet dry. Choose waterproof socks and/or stop regularly to change into dry socks so your skin does not soften and be prone to peeling/blistering. At worst, you might develop trench foot (*see* page 130) or other infections. Air your feet when you can and use foot powder or Hydropel ointment to dry them at transitions.

3. Invest in good socks. Buy dedicated socks that fit your feet well, breathe freely and wick moisture away from the skin. The fewer the seams, the better. Teflon patches or dual layering further reduce the risk of blisters.

4. Keep your feet clean. When you feel debris in your shoe, stop and remove it before the friction causes a 'hot spot' that is sure to lead to a blister. Clean any grit off your feet when you change shoes.

5. Swap your shoes. Change shoes every time you get to a transition area, allowing the used pair to be aired until you next meet up with your support crew. This necessitates two pairs of shoes, one of which could be a bigger size to allow for swelling later in the race.

6. Get your feet up. When you rest, lie back and elevate your feet to reduce blood pressure and the swelling that goes hand in hand with monster trekking legs.

7. Use the right shoe for the job. Wearing water shoes or booties on a paddling leg keeps trekking shoes dry, and the improved insulation keeps your feet from freezing. Bike shoes were not made for walking, so rather pack your trekking shoes if you expect a huge push during the mountain-biking leg.

8. Prevent blisters. Isolate 'hot spots' with Moleskinz™ plasters or cushioning bandages. If blisters do appear, deal with them as soon as possible. Drain the fluid and inject with methyalide to prevent infection. If this does not help and the blister spreads, wrap the affected area tightly in adhesive or duct tape.

9. Take up your trekking poles. If used correctly, poles will reduce the load on your feet by proportionally redistributing it to arms and shoulders. This reduces wear and tear. As balancing tools, they avoid twisted ankles and other injuries.

10. Train and stretch. Include your feet in your stretching regime, ensuring strong and supple foot muscles. This improves your balance and could go a long way towards minimizing repetitive stress injuries.

Adapted from information supplied by adventure racer, Ugene Nel

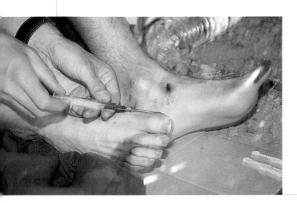

TOP: Use foot powder to minimize moisture and the risk of your feet becoming infected.
ABOVE: Drain blisters of fluid and inject with methyalide to prevent infection.
RIGHT: Foot stretches are vital to ensure strong, supple feet.

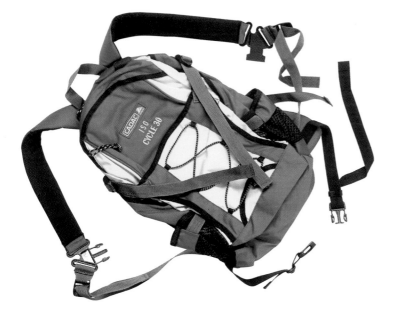

The perfect pack

It is difficult to be objective when it comes to selecting the perfect pack for adventure racing; most athletes have personal favourites. Stability and comfort will influence your decision. Does the pack suit you anatomically, is it a snug fit without bounce or sway, is it stable when carried, are the shoulder straps anatomically shaped or do they cause any chafing? Ensure that the pack does not cause shoulder or hip 'hot spots', which are precursors to blisters.

Once you have answered these questions satisfactorily, weight will be the next determining factor for some, while others may prefer to consider functionality and design. How easy will it be to access gear on the fly? What is the total pack volume? How many litres of water can your hydration system hold? Does the pack include features such as a shock cord system, trekking pole slots, compression straps, a sternum strap with bottle holders, mesh hip belt pockets, a stowable rain cover or a detachable chest map pouch? Durable fabric (usually a Cordura ripstop or nylon variant) and bombproof construction (double-stitched seams, YKK zips, double-layered base, etc.) also score major points.

As a rule of thumb, the longer the race distance, the bigger the pack. Sprint races are generally not gear-intensive so you can get away with a pack volume of 10–15 litres. For weekender and classic distances, pack size will increase to about 30-litres, while true expedition races within alpine environments might see you carrying up to 50 litres. The bigger the pack you carry, the more gear you will carry. You do not need lots of extra pockets, tabs and buckles; keep it light and simple.

An important consideration is multi-functionality, so make sure your pack works as well on the

Backpack portage

strap is loose and pack is hanging away from the body

chest strap needs tightening

Incorrect

back pack fits snugly

chest strap is tightened

Correct

TOP: **Choose a pack that is suited to your anatomical proportions.**

ABOVE: **When your chest and hip belt has been correctly adjusted, weight will be effectively distributed between your shoulders and hips.**

Backpack features

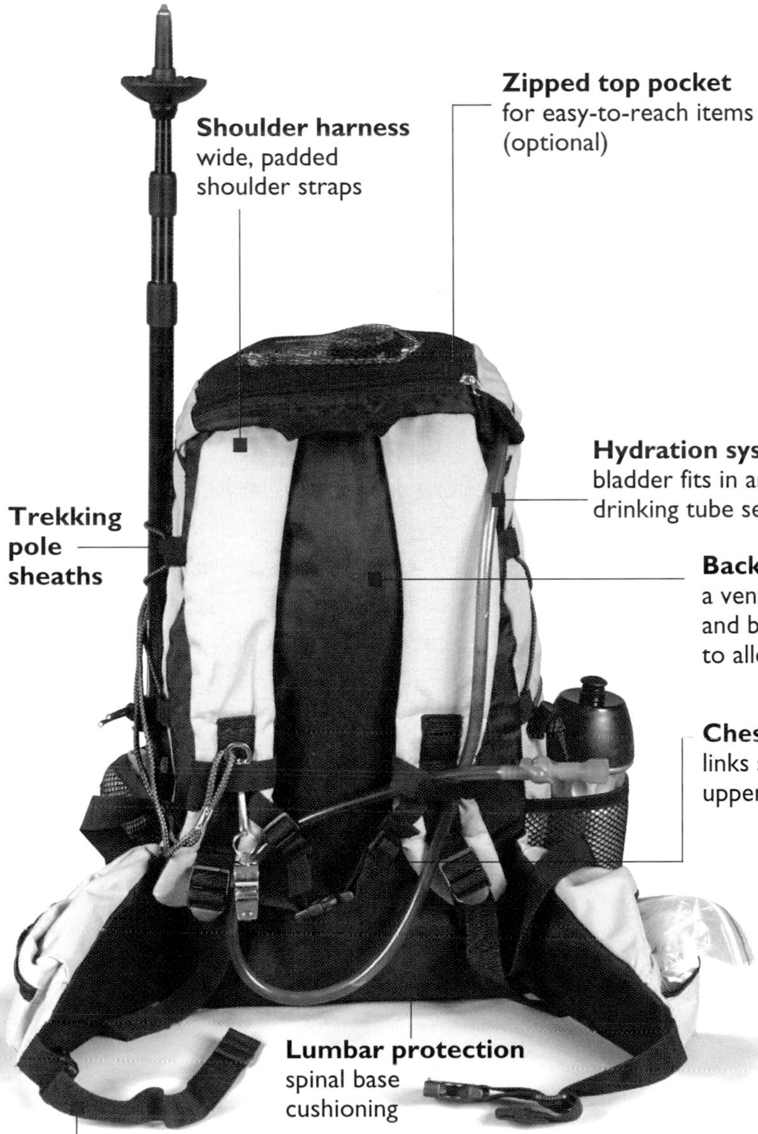

Shoulder harness
wide, padded
shoulder straps

Zipped top pocket
for easy-to-reach items
(optional)

Trekking pole sheaths

Hydration system
bladder fits in an internal pocket and
drinking tube secures to harness

Back system
a ventilation tunnel for airflow
and breathable mesh material
to allow quick drying

Chest strap
links shoulder straps across
upper chest

Lumbar protection
spinal base
cushioning

Hip belt
fitted cut to protect hips
during heavy load carrying

Grab handle
convenient
handhold for
lifting backpack

Shock cord carry system
to secure helmet or
other items

Mesh side pockets

Hip belt pocket
for on-the-move storage

Mesh storage pockets
elasticized outside storage
for wet/messy/constant-use items

Compression strap
use to adjust the
volume of your pack to
suit your load

trekking legs as it does on mountain biking sections. Even better, an elasticized rain cover will make it splashproof when paddling as well. Maintain a cool body temperature by choosing a back system incorporating mesh or tunnelling to allow airflow between the pack and your body. A shaped harness and belt system will add comfort during all-day slogs. Also make sure your pack can be adjusted 'on the fly', thus avoiding time-wasting stops.

Colour is a personal choice: earthy tones allow you to slip away from other teams, while bright colours allow evacuation helicopters to locate you easily. Consider this in conjunction with technical specifications, durability, price and after-sales service. If possible, borrow a range of packs from friends and fellow racers and field-test them before making a decision. The multitude of well-known brands from major international manufacturers allows you to weigh up the various pros and cons until you find a pack that perfectly suits your body and racing requirements.

The longer the race, the heavier the weight you will have to carry – except for stage races. This makes sense, but there are various factors that might influence the weight an individual will carry within a team. For example, to keep a navigator or trail-finder fresh, members might decide to lighten his or her load. Adventure racing requires you to race as light as possible; the heavier your pack, the more it will influence your rhythm, balance and posture.

When packing, weight should be evenly distributed throughout the pack, although many racers prefer a lower centre of gravity, with heavy items at the bottom. Pack often-needed items on top. (*See the photograph opposite for what items to pack where.*) A clip-lock chest strap reduces bounce and helps to keep the pack from dragging your shoulders back, encouraging the correct upright posture. When packing, remember that no pack is ever 100 per cent waterproof. In fact, lack of drainage may

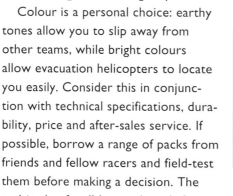

> **Tip**
> Line your pack with a 'bin liner' type bag. If it rains, your pack will get wet but your kit inside will remain dry.

pose a major problem during canyoning, water crossings or in a rainforest race. Rather choose a pack that has drainage holes and mesh panels to allow water that collects inside to escape and use Ziploc™ or garbage bags to keep key items dry inside, while utilizing your splash cover to keep rain out. Water crossings might necessitate more extreme waterproofing measures, and survival bags are often used to float gear across dams, lakes or rivers.

Additional gear items

To simplify your gear purchases further, this section lists some other important kit items not previously covered in detail. The list has been kept concise and generally mountain biking and trekking related, as all these items, as well as other technical gear, will be covered in detailed sections on the various individual disciplines in Chapter Five.

The list includes: trekking poles, sleeping bags, shelters or bivvy bags (in extreme cases, tents might be specified), headlamps, cycling gear (bike, helmet, gloves, clothing, tools, tyre liners, spare tubes, repair kit, light, reflector), water bottles, emergency equipment (whistle, knife, waterproof matches, survival blanket, rope, flare kit, Lumisticks), a first-aid kit (for contents, see page 155) as well as navigational and orienteering equipment (see pages 100–102 for more).

Now get cracking and start packing!

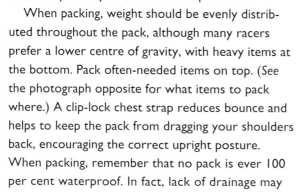

TOP: **Share the load if you see that one of your team members is battling to cope with the pace during a section of the race.**

ABOVE LEFT: **Dry-bags are great to keep gear dry, but may be too bulky for race use.**

What goes where

Zipped top pocket
navigational kit, sunglasses and other fragile items you might need on a regular basis

Internal bladder sleeve
holds your hydration system bladder

Main compartment
spare clothes, sleeping bag, tubes, first-aid kit, emergency rations, warm clothes close to the top

Shock cord carry system
helmet, rolled-up maps, pump, warm fleece, hat

Hip belt pocket
race food, plasters, sunscreen, energy gels, multi-tool

Hip belt pocket
race food, sunscreen, energy gels, plasters, multi-tool

Elasticized side pockets
water bottles with supplements or electrolytes

Mesh compartment
wet socks and gear, gloves, flare, things you might need along the way

List of forbidden equipment Ø

Weapons of any description • Any mode of transport except for that supplied by event organizers • Global Positioning System (GPS) unit • Night vision equipment • Any maps other than those supplied by event organizers • Radios or unsealed mobile phones other than those supplied by event organizers

ABOVE: Every individual athlete has his or her preferred way of packing for the race, but the guidelines given in the labelled photograph above should provide some handy suggestions. Event experience will help you decide what to pack where.

AR
disciplines

To **COMPETE SUCCESSFULLY** during even the most basic adventure race, you must be proficient in a range of sporting disciplines. This chapter touches on some of these activities – some well known and others more obscure. It also discusses some of the skills required, reviews equipment and clothing you might need, and gets some of the world's top racers to share their AR know-how.

As you can expect to spend the bulk of the race on either your feet or your bike, many athletes tend to focus most of their training on this. It would, however, be a grave oversight to leave paddling out of the pre-race build-up; upper-body strength, balance and water skills are imperative, and a lack of relevant training could therefore quite easily scupper your chances of finishing the race. Cross-training will not only help you to cope with the muscle strain you will face during individual disciplines, but will ensure your body can cope with the transition between diverse activities such as cycling and running or swimming. With training comes confidence. Each time you do an abseil or eskimo roll, your mind will dissect the physiological sequence and log it somewhere in your brain, ready to retrieve the data when you are faced with the same challenge during the race. Know one thing, though: no matter how well you prepare, when the organizer throws in an unexpected curved ball, you will have to think on your feet.

Arm yourself with information about:

1 Trekking and trail running ✓

2 Mountain biking ✓

3 Paddling techniques ✓

4 Mountaineering and rope work ✓

5 Coping with desert environments and sub-zero temperatures ✓

6 Other AR disciplines, such as:

   Canyoning ✓

   Coasteering ✓

   Open-water swimming ✓

   Horseback riding and pack animals ✓

   In-line (speed) skating ✓

   Traditional craft ✓

TOP: **Competitors prepare themselves for one of the adventure legs during the exciting Land Rover G4 Challenge in the Western Cape, South Africa.**
INSET: **The buzz of anticipation at the start is the drug of choice for adventure racers.**

1. Trekking and trail running

One of the few things you can be certain of when lining up at the start of a race is that you will spend a sizeable segment of any adventure race on your feet. Expect this to be very different from running a marathon along an even road surface, though; fancy footwork is required to negotiate anything from mountain trekking or dune running to scrambling and rock hopping.

You will also need to cope with a range of challenging surfaces by adapting your stride, balance, rhythm and posture. Every variation in terrain comes with its own challenges and your running technique will have to change in order to move forward at an efficient pace (see 'Terrain techniques' on page 48). Most importantly, your gear and especially your footwear must be suited to the race terrain, helping you safely negotiate sand, rock, scree, marshland and stream beds, or whatever else might lie between you and the finish line.

Spending time on your feet during training is key to doing well during the race; improve your on-the-ground skills by taking on testing terrain to get both mind and body into the right groove. Also keep in mind that any race stretching beyond 150km (93 miles) will see you venturing into pack-animal territory, so get used to dealing with a 8–12kg (18–26 lb) pack early on during your training runs.

Train your brain to be constantly aware of your posture and balance while carrying your pack, literally 'thinking' your ankles, knees, arms and torso through treacherous terrain until every movement becomes second nature to you. Although every individual tends to have a unique approach, it will not hurt to watch what others do and to adapt your technique accordingly.

Effective use of energy is imperative, so find your own zone where pace, breathing and speed of advance settle into a safe equilibrium.

ABOVE RIGHT: Balance is the key to forward movement; scan the terrain ahead of you as you run so that you can relay information about the route, as well as any obstacles you discover, back to the other members of your team.

Terrain techniques

Keep these tips and techniques in mind when taking your first steps into the off-road world of AR. Rather start off cautiously and increase the momentum as your confidence grows, but remember that you are part of a team, so the slowest member should set the pace. A good idea is to let the strongest member scout ahead in order to find the easiest route, saving the others from expending unnecessary energy. (Note that winter terrain is discussed in detail on pages 70–72.)

SINGLE-TRACK
Terrain: A narrow trail traversing the natural landscape
Topography: Mountains, plains and everything in-between
Surface: Varies between compact hard-pack, sandy stretches and stable, surface bedrock

Obstacles: Log or stone steps, loose stones on footpath, tree roots, overhanging branches, etc.
Stride length: Normal, but varies depending on terrain, gradient and surface
Posture: Upright with elbows out and arms slightly lifted to help maintain balance
Tip: Get the frontrunner to warn those at the rear of any looming obstacles

SAND
Terrain: Arid deserts around the world, unspoilt beaches and dry riverbeds
Topography: Towering dunes to flat, coastal plains stretching along the shoreline
Surface: From knee-deep, wind-blown drifts to firm, wet sand within the marine tidal zone

Obstacles: Loose sand drifts, concealed rocks and branches, extreme temperatures
Stride length: Shorter than normal with a shuffling gait; very short when ascending dunes, bounding downhill
Posture: Vary from an on-all-fours crawl on the ascent to weight slightly back when descending
Tip: Tape up your socks and wear gaiters to keep the sand out of your shoes

CANYONING AND COASTEERING
Terrain: Inland rivers and streams; stretches of rocky coastline anywhere on the ocean
Topography: Jagged cliffs, smooth boulders, waterfalls, slippery rocks, wet sand
Surface: Vertical and slippery rock faces, miles of treacherous boulders, rock-strewn beaches

ABOVE: **A team descends along the ridge of a massive dune during the Desert Challenge, scouting for the best route through the vast Namib Desert. Opt for compact sand, often found in lower-lying gullies or to the leeward side of dunes.**

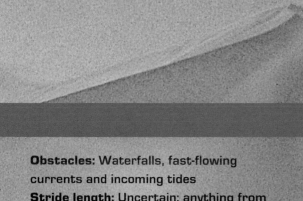

Obstacles: Waterfalls, fast-flowing currents and incoming tides

Stride length: Uncertain; anything from 2m (6ft) rock jumps to inching through a chest-deep river

Posture: Anything goes from running, jumping, wading, hiking and crawling to contortionist teetering

Tip: Waterproof yourself and your essential kit (and always remember to pack a dry set of clothing and socks)

ABOVE: During any race, the terrain will often dictate your speed of advance. Adapt your posture, stride length and pace to suit thick brush, snow, mud, scree slopes, rocks and other natural obstacles.

Desert trekking tips

During the 1998 Eco-Challenge in Morocco, I was faced by many factors I do not usually encounter when racing in Scandinavia, where I was born. Racers from northern climates should keep the following in mind:

WATER

When the temperature is around 40°C (104°F), your body uses much more water than normal. Plan in advance and identify water resupply points on your map before starting. Purify water along the way if necessary and compensate for the loss of salts and minerals by drinking electrolytes to prevent cramping.

TEMPERATURE

In the desert, there is a massive difference between daytime and night-time temperatures. Always pack a survival blanket and, if you plan to camp overnight, bring a tent or bivvy and sleeping bag no matter the daytime temperature.

ULTRAVIOLET PROTECTION

Always wear sunscreen, breathable, lightweight clothing and a hat and sunglasses to protect you from the sun.

SHOES AND SOCKS

Use a good pair of shoes that have been properly walked in and tested. Avoid double-layer socks, which collect sand between the outer and inner layer, causing ballooning hot spots that can soon lead to friction blisters. Avoid Achilles tendon problems by inserting small pads inside shoes to raise heels by approximately 1cm, thus protecting them from stress while walking in sand.

NAVIGATION

Look at the map twice as often as usual; there are few obvious features to help you orient yourself and your compass navigation has to be spot on.

TREKKING POLES

Always use trekking poles to redistribute some body weight to your arms, shoulders and upper body. This will save your legs, which will probably already be suffering from the added energy you will be expending in the soft, sandy terrain.

Johan Andersson, Team Silva

cap with flap

survival blanket

RailRider™

water purification tablets

trekking pole

ABOVE LEFT: Major hazards when trekking through the desert are sandstorms. Pack a Buff™ or another garment to cover your face and, if you suspect that you may have lost your way, wait it out and scout for recognizable landmarks.

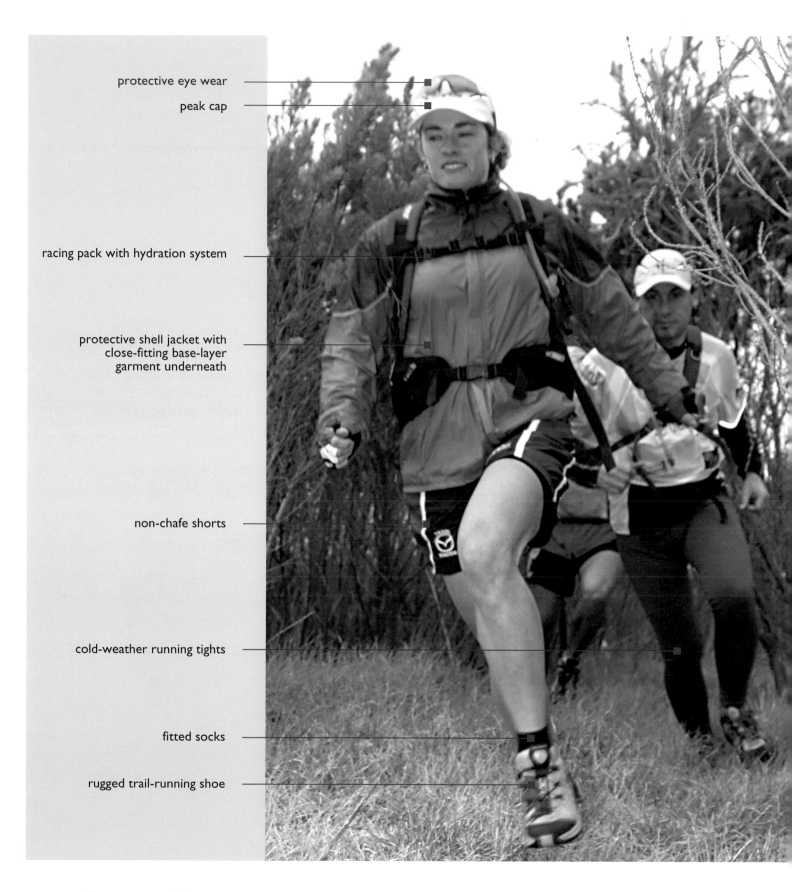

protective eye wear

peak cap

racing pack with hydration system

protective shell jacket with
close-fitting base-layer
garment underneath

non-chafe shorts

cold-weather running tights

fitted socks

rugged trail-running shoe

ABOVE: Choose your trekking and trail-running gear with care, and make sure every item
is well tested before the race. Special attention should be paid to shoes, which must be
suited to your foot shape and running style.

2. Mountain biking

Although you spend most of your race time doing the long, hard trekking slog, the discipline that invariably allows you to cover the most ground during a race is mountain biking. It is therefore no wonder that team members are often quizzed on their biking skills before their proficiency in other racing disciplines is checked. Anything goes during AR cycling legs. Depending on the race region, you might be faced with tortuous climbs, rocky portages, hair-raising downhills, mud-sucking marsh pushing or high-speed gravel flats. See '10 terrain tips' opposite for handy advice on how to handle these surface variations.

When covering ground fast, expect to wipe out sooner rather than later, so ensure you know how to fall: clip out, slide, aim for the least dangerous impact zone, tuck in your arms and roll. Consider attending a weekend mountain-biking clinic to hone your advanced riding skills, which include anything from bunny-hopping obstacles to controlled sliding along a treacherous downhill. Your bike frame and components must be set up to suit your physical proportions, thus ensuring comfortable cranking. For the best way of doing this, see the diagram below.

Sizing body to bike frame

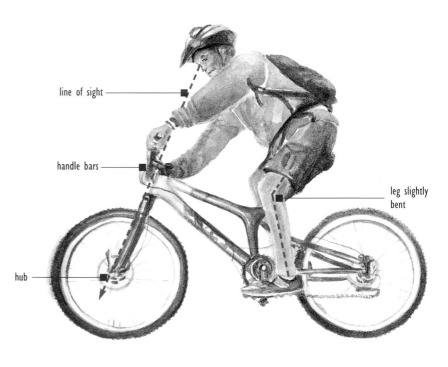

line of sight

handle bars

leg slightly bent

hub

ABOVE LEFT: Learn to distribute your weight correctly for greater balance and stability.
ABOVE RIGHT: When sitting comfortably on the saddle with both feet on the pedals and arms slightly bent, your angle of view should line the handle bars up with your front wheel cog.

10 terrain tips

1. MUD
Fit shed-tread tyres to avoid a surface build-up of mud and install a crud-catcher to keep tyre-splatter out of your eyes. Opt for the route of least resistance and maintain momentum. Also, save time by washing your bike before the gunk hardens.

2. SAND
Wider, softer tyres stop you from slicing into sand and improve front wheel control. Gear down and sit back in the saddle, positioning weight over the rear wheel to increase traction. Steer as straight a route as possible, allowing the rear tyre to follow the line of the front wheel if you can.

3. WATER
If you have time, scout the crossing on foot — you never know what lurks below the surface. Otherwise hit it at speed, gearing down to crank through the increased resistance of the water and lifting yourself off the saddle for balance. Glasses will keep your vision clear.

4. TREE ROOTS
Try to hit these at right angles to avoid front-wheel deflection along the line of the root, which would pitch you over the handlebars. Dip down hard on the front fork just before impact to 'pop' your front wheel over the thicker ones and move forward off the saddle when your rear wheel crosses.

5. LOGS
Similar technique to navigating tree roots, with you hitting the log at a 90° angle. You will probably need more height to clear the obstacle, so lift and lunge your front wheel, using the chain ring to crank the bike across. If you know your story, go the bunny-hop route and clear trees in one grand bound.

6. SNOW AND ICE
Let some air out of tyres to improve traction and opt for an aggressive tread pattern. Balance is key, but be ready to clip out of the pedal and dab (touch your feet on the ground) as you slide into corners.

7. ROCKS
The more momentum you have, the smoother the ride. Use the suspension to soak up the hits, but stick to your line once you have made your decision. Harder tyres will not add to a comfortable ride, but will help to avoid snake-bite flats (*see* page 90).

8. LOOSE SURFACE GRAVEL
Inconsistent contact between your tyres and an uncertain surface spells danger, so be steady and deliberate in your movements. Practise controlled sliding by feathering and/or locking the front and rear brakes in unison.

9. DROP-OFFS
Get your butt way back off the saddle to move your weight off the front fork and stop it from bottoming out and throwing you over the top. Alternatively, power off at speed and drop in on your rear wheel.

10. NARROW GAPS
Rule number one: relax! Rule number two: do not look at the obstacle; somehow the front wheel always follows the line of sight. Rather fix your gaze on a spot a short distance beyond the gap and keep pedalling.

ABOVE RIGHT: The better you get to know your bike, the easier it will be to handle mud, logs or hard pack at high speed. Speed is your friend; you will ride over most obstacles if you keep your speed up.

Equipment

Whether or not you are an experienced mountain biker, you will have to carry your bike at some stage of the race. Weight is therefore one good reason why you should invest in a hard-tail; not only is it easier on your shoulders during the portages, you also carry less weight when you go head to head with gravity along any hard-core climbs. Fork out for front suspension to improve handling and reduce shoulder and arm stress, and for a lightweight and solid frame and durable wheel sets. Good bike lights – either bar- or helmet-mounted (or head-lamp) – are a must. In addition, most racers fit a bar-bag to allow them on-the-move access to food and other key items. Nav-boards (basically perspex clipboards mounted to the handlebars via a swivel mount) make navigation easy, while other AR modifications might include on-the-fly towing assemblies to allow team members to hook up their bike to a stronger cyclist by means of a bungy cord.

bungy cord

Before you line up at the start, make sure your bike has been properly serviced and your wheels have been puncture-proofed with slime or tyre liners; in some areas, you might need both. You should also be fully kitted out with a pump and the necessary tools to help you cope with unexpected emergencies along the way. See your tubby bag as your bike's on-board emergency kit – it should be able to handle most on-trail repairs without being crammed full. First on the list is a quality multi-tool that works; functions should include screwdrivers (stars and flats), a blade, pliers, a selection of Allen-keys, spanners and wrenches (choose a separate chain breaker, which usually works better). Other must-haves include a spare inner tube, puncture kit, emergency cash stash (you never know . . .), tube of lubricant and a few plasters. As for your backpack, use the same one as on the trekking legs, ensuring it has at least a chest strap, hip belt, easy-to-reach belt pockets and an expandable helmet-carrying system. Carry about one litre (2pt) of water for every hour on the trail; add potions/electrolytes/supplements as you see fit, but do not try something new during a race. Energy snacks, additional inner tubes, gloves, a sweatband, a windproof shell jacket, sunscreen and eye protection should be packed within easy reach.

Clothing

Mountain biking requires more than regulation trekking togs, although your base layer (plus fleece and/or shell) will still protect you against the elements. You need padded cycling shorts, dedicated socks, a protective cycling helmet (preferably a fusion, in-mould microshell unit with venting, adjustable peak visor and CE/EN and CPSC safety ratings) and clip-in mountain-biking shoes. SPD shoes (a generic term that evolved from the term Shimano Pedalling Dynamics) maximize pedalling efficiency through clipping into a quick-release mechanism on the pedal so you can pull on the upstroke. A solid fastening system, a well-padded tongue, and a rigid, reinforced mid-sole with just enough flex for when you have to get off and push will make for a comfortable fit and good power transfer to the pedals. Wear padded gloves to stop your hands going numb.

TIP

If the entire team uses tubes with the same valve type, it saves having to carry different pumps and tubes. Also use the same type and length of spoke.

bicycle pump

ABOVE LEFT: **Tie-down bungy cords or retractable dog leashes can be modified for mountain-bike towing, and no-one should venture out without a bicycle pump.**
ABOVE RIGHT: **Clip a navigation board to your handle bars to improve map reading.**

cycling gloves

protective helmet

adventure racing backpack
with hydration system

padded cycling
shorts

lightweight bike
frame (full sus-
pension or
hard-tail)

fitted socks

clip-in (or SPD)
mountain-
biking shoes

ABOVE: **A lightweight bike frame should be complemented by comfortable, clip-in shoes,
a well-ventilated helmet and protective gloves. Never forget to carry a cycling tool kit
to help you cope with on-trail emergencies.**

3. Aqua action

This chapter cannot cover in detail the range of paddling disciplines you will encounter during your AR adventures. In fact, a separate book could scarcely cover options as diverse as rafting, kayaking and canoeing (plus some additional, non-paddling activities such as hydro-boarding and pack-rafting). And this is only the tip of the iceberg: each individual discipline needs to be approached differently, depending on the water conditions within which you will be paddling. If you are at sea, what will the size of the swell be? When on a river, can you expect it to be flat or will you duel with Grade 5 rapids along the way? Fresh water lakes can come with or without wind, posing an endless stream (excuse the pun) of decisions.

Craft types

Once you know what type of aqua adventure you are in for, you are faced with an astounding array of possible watercraft choices, ranging from sleek Kevlar™ kayaks to PVC rafts with about as much drag as the Titanic. Take kayaks as an example: these alone may be divided further into at least a dozen classes. Choose between either traditional sit-in boats or more stable, sit-on versions. Then take your pick from singles, doubles or triples, folding kayaks, sectional kayaks or even inflatables. Design features, such as the chine (shape), beam and length of the hull, the angle of the keel and rockers, the material used in manufacturing the craft, the type of steering mechanism, cockpit configuration, weight and volume, will determine the handling and overall stability of the kayak. You are really faced, then, with a 'horses for courses' scenario: extreme whitewater

TOP: **A reasonable level of skill is required to negotiate pounding surf close to the shore. Maintain forward motion through powerful strokes and lean back to prevent the prow from dipping underwater.**

rivers might necessitate inflatable, two-person rafts that basically go with the flow, while milder waters such as calm lakes or a flat ocean would be suited to long and narrow craft, usually manufactured from a fibre-composite material. Generally, fibre-glass is the most affordable option, but Kevlar™ and carbon fibres are used to produce featherlight and extremely rigid – albeit more expensive – craft. Their sleek finish and tapered lines make for excellent tracking and speed, although the narrow beam renders them relatively unstable. Always check inside the hatches of a composite boat to give you a good idea of build quality. Apply a UV protective marine coating a few times a year to protect it from the sun. Plastics (boats made from polyethylene) are great for rocky coastlines and shallow watercourses as they will handle the inevitable bump and grind, but the downside is that they are heavier and less rigid, and they exhibit increased drag, making them slower in the water.

Clearly, then, there is no 'perfect' craft for adventure racing. Your choice will be determined largely by water conditions, weather forecasts, leg distances, your personal level of skill, and craft specifications in the official race rules. In many of the series aimed at beginners and intermediate racers, event organizers supply boats for the water legs or clearly specify exact craft requirements.

If you do decide to take your own boat, ensure it conforms to these specifications. For example, there might be a limitation on the ratio between the beam

width and the length of the craft to ensure fair competition when it comes to speed. Restricting the beam to not less than 1/10th the length of the boat – so 55cm wide for a 5.5m boat – also makes for a more stable boat that can handle heavy swells, even with a less skilful paddler at the helm. Hybrid kayaks combine the stability and ease of use of sit-on boats with traditional craft's good tracking and protection against exposure; they are therefore a good compromise. Check your craft can comfortably carry the equipment you require during the race and that the stow-holds and watertight hatches will keep your gear dry.

TOP: **Choose your craft carefully; you may have to carry it. Consider using portage wheels.**
ABOVE: **The variety of craft is enormous. From left: fibreglass canoes, plastic river kayaks, aluminium open canoes, an inflatable raft, inflatable kayak and double sea kayak.**

Water skills

Acquiring a boat is much easier than gaining the skills to handle your craft competently; these cannot be purchased at your local outdoor store and need to be honed during years of on-the-water practice. Your paddling stroke will vary greatly depending on your craft and the water conditions, but some general rules apply nonetheless (see 'Paddling tips for all water craft' on page 62). As you become more skilled, you will confidently add manoeuvres – such as the pry, the draw, the sweep, bracing, stern rudder drags or the reverse stroke – to your repertoire of paddling strokes. Keep your upper body stable and concentrate on rhythmic, even strokes in sync with your breathing, entering your blade into the water as close to the boat as possible and at right angles to your direction of travel.

Execute the stroke itself in a fashion similar to digging a spade into soil; while you draw back against the water, use your opposite hand to push the paddle through its arc. Two easy ways of becoming a more proficient paddler are to join an experienced athlete for a few open-water sessions or to attend a paddling clinic. Major event organizers present clinics regularly, and details are easily available on AR chat forums or from related web resources. 'Reading' a river or a body of water is another skill you will acquire as you become more versed in the various aquatic disciplines. If you are unsure of a paddling section and suspect danger ahead, make every effort to scout before paddling it; if you are in any doubt as to your safety, rather carry your boat until you reach safe water again. Constantly be aware – look and listen for variations in the water characteristics as you move down a river or across the ocean, as conditions might change with little warning.

TOP: **Keeping yourself and your gear as warm and dry as possible will conserve energy and make for more comfortable paddling.**
ABOVE LEFT: **The concave blade on a wing paddle increases stroke efficiency.**

If you are headed for an unknown river, use your map and calculate the gradient of river – how many metres or feet the river descends per kilometre/mile – to give an indication of the conditions to expect: less than 1m/km (5ft/mile) forecasts a tame river; a drop of up to 10m/km equates to moderate rapids; but expect waterfalls and severe rapids at anything from 10–70m/km.

You should be proficient in a range of skills before you take on any serious paddle, the first of these being the ability to get back into your kayak if you fall out. Re-entry techniques are critical to your survival so practise them in calm water before you take any watercraft out for the first time.

Recovery through executing the Eskimo roll (named after the Inuit people who perfected so as to spend as little time as possible in Arctic waters) is the most effective way of righting your kayak after you have tipped over. Most people tend to panic once their heads are plunged under water, but you have at least 45 seconds before you need your next breath. Do not panic. Think through the basic rolling technique (see diagrams below), moving your torso as flat against the stern as possible and flicking through the roll with your hips. The same goes for self-rescue techniques, assisted rescues involving other boats, towing and the like: practice makes perfect, so if at first you do not succeed, try and try again.

Hazards to watch for:

- **whirlpools:** usually found where the water course suddenly widen
- **siphons:** where the current flows through or under boulders or potholes, causing a suction effect
- **standing waves:** a wave breaking upriver, usually beyond a massive, submerged rock or hole
- **strainers:** where the river forces its way through overhanging branches, fences or dead trees
- **lateral waves:** coming off obstructions or river features at an angle to the water flow
- **hydraulics, or holes:** a reversal of flow (see standing waves) where variable flow speeds force some water back upstream
- **keepers:** holes through which water constantly recycles and which may hold you down indefinitely – referred to as 'washing machines'
- **eddies:** areas of relative calm protected by an upriver obstacle.

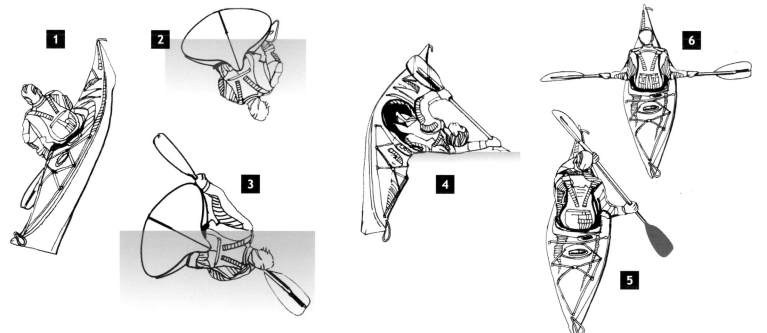

How to execute an eskimo roll

1. Set up the paddle in the 'wind-up' position. Hold this position as you turn upside down. 2. Orientate yourself and set up for the sweep, knocking the rear blade against the craft to ensure it is raised correctly. 3. Sweep the forward blade toward the rear, keeping it close to the surface initially and then leaning on it to start the hip flick. 4. The hip flick should turn the kayak enough for its own buoyancy to help with the raise. Lean back and raise your head last. 5. Once up, steady yourself to avoid recapsizing.

Equipment

If you have any money left after splashing out on your boat, add the following priority items to your shopping list: a paddle, a personal flotation device (PFD), a throw-line and a spray-deck. Without a paddle (generally a composite of fibreglass, resin and carbon fibres, sometimes with an aluminium or wooden shaft) you will be up the proverbial creek; choose a lightweight, rigid 'blade' suited to your craft and approximately 1.25 times your height.

A good tip from racer Chad Ulansky is to check the length of your paddle by standing next to the upright paddle; if you can curl your fingers around the tip of the blade at the top, it should work just fine. Wing-shaped paddles (with concave blades) give improved thrust, but the more conventional, symmetrically shaped blades allow you more control during manoeuvring strokes. The off-set angle between the blades is referred to as 'feathering'; in some higher-priced models, this – and the length of the shaft – may be adjusted to suit individual body, water and wind dynamics.

Safety is imperative, so a good PFD is non-negotiable. Even though it will not float you right-side up when unconscious, it will assist in flotation during an emergency. Crotch straps (to keep it from riding up when in the water), bright colours (to increase your visibility during rescue operations), adjustable fit (to avoid chafing) and mesh pockets all add value to an item that might save your life.

marine compass

Protect your lower body from the elements in a sit-in (closed cockpit) or hybrid kayak by wearing a spray-deck. This is usually manufactured from stretchy neoprene or nylon fabric that fits snugly around your waist and fastens around the cockpit coaming (raised lip) in order to keep water out of the boat. Ensure it is fitted with easy-release loops, allowing you to 'pop' the deck in case of a wet exit where you cannot execute a roll to right the kayak.

A good throw-line is also useful during rescue or towing. Other items you might want to consider include a hydration pack to allow you to drink on the move, a bilge pump, dry-bag, on-board compass, protective head gear (a helmet is a must in whitewater rivers) and sunscreen lotion.

Clothing

A neoprene wetsuit might be required as the first line of protection in cold waters. Depending on the temperature and wind chill, decide between a full wet- or drysuit with a hood, booties and gloves or, if the weather is milder, a short-sleeved suit with a paddling jacket.

You may require little more than a quick-drying, thermal base layer top (cut longer so it does not ride up), a protective wind-shell jacket, a cap with a neck-flap and enough sunscreen to keep the UV rays at bay. Sunglasses are a must to protect your eyes against glare and salt spray, while gloves will guard against ulcerated hands.

paddle

spray-deck

hydration pack

paddling jacket

personal flotation device (PFD)

ABOVE: Once you have splashed out on your boat, you still have to budget for items such as an on-board compass, a basic paddle, a spray-deck, a hydration pack, and a PFD, before you are ready to take to the water in a race.

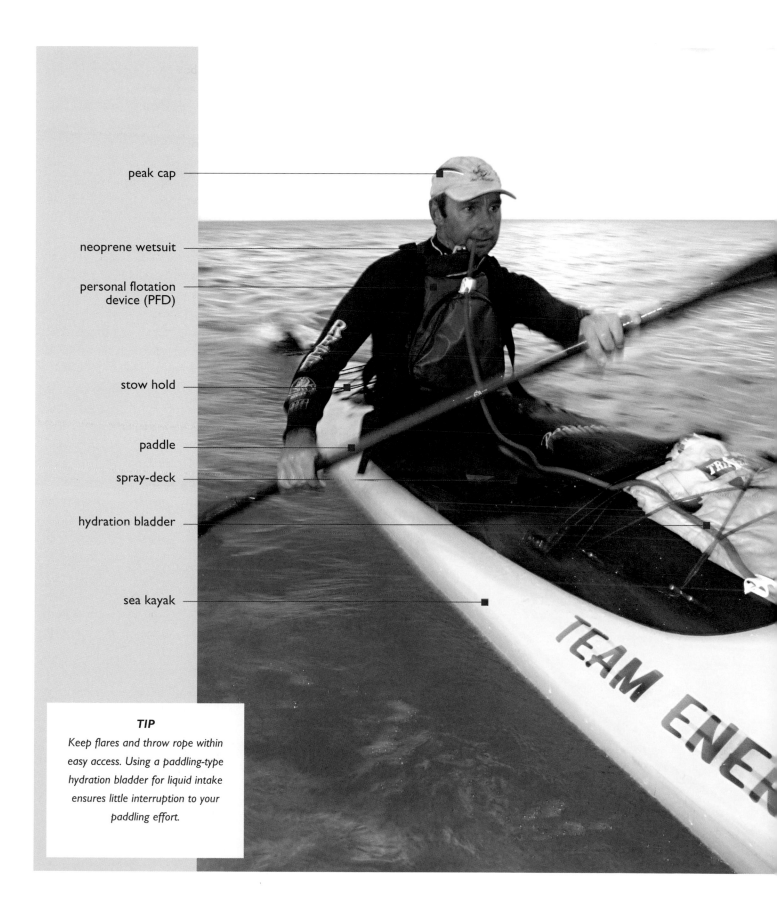

peak cap

neoprene wetsuit

personal flotation device (PFD)

stow hold

paddle

spray-deck

hydration bladder

sea kayak

TIP
Keep flares and throw rope within easy access. Using a paddling-type hydration bladder for liquid intake ensures little interruption to your paddling effort.

ABOVE: **Sea kayaks come in all shapes and sizes; the craft you choose should be suited to the actual paddling conditions you will experience during the race, as well as to your personal water skills level.**

Paddling technique

Most North American adventure athletes have very poor paddling technique, especially when kayaking. One reason is the lack of competitive kayak races – canoe races are much more common in all states except Hawaii, Florida, Texas and California. Here are some useful tips.

1. In the forward power stroke, do not favour the biceps as the primary power source; use all torso muscles and, to a lesser extent, the hips and legs.

2. Do not flex your arms too much (no more than 30°). Keep your arms locked at the elbow and provide all the movement by rotating your torso, starting at the waist.

3. To start the stroke, rotate your body fully to one side so your chest faces at least 45° from its neutral position as you sit in the boat. Keeping your forward arm fully extended (and straight), push the paddle blade down into the water. This 'catch' phase of your stroke is where you start to exert forward power.

4. For the 'dive' or 'power' phase, rotate your torso back through neutral to a full 45° to the other side. Think of pulling the boat forward, and lean downward slightly on your paddle at the start of the drive. Keep arms straight and let the paddle move sideways away from the boat as it nears the 'exit' phase.

5. For the exit, pull the paddle from the water out to the side (at right angles to the direction of movement of the boat), starting around your hip. Avoid pulling the paddle blade too far back or you lose power and start to lift water as the blade becomes horizontal. Keep splash from the paddle to a minimum.

Paddling tips for all watercraft

1. Aim to strike waves at a 90° angle.

2. Avoid as many waves, rocks and other obstructions as possible – they slow you down.

3. Always tether your paddle to your watercraft.

4. When faced with obstructions, keep paddling until you are well clear.

5. As you approach a hole or hydraulic, avoid shying away, which will make you tip; instead, lean *into* the water's force and paddle through it.

6. If you fall out, make yourself as small as possible; thrashing extends your surface area and wastes energy.

7. Hold your paddle so that you have 90° angles at your elbows. To find the correct position, put the paddle on top of your head and place your hands on it so that they are directly over your elbows.

8. Balance is key to paddling success; keeping your torso stable ensures a powerful stroke.

Based on Don Mann and Kara Schaad's
The Complete Guide to Adventure Racing

6. As you perform the forward power stroke with one paddle blade, the other blade is moving through the 'return' stroke. Starting at the exit point, lift the returning blade into the air as the drive blade starts its catch. Keep your return arm mostly straight, and punch forward in front of your face as the drive hand goes through the power phase of the stroke.

7. Always keep the paddle shaft between 30° and 45° from vertical while the paddle is in the water; do not lunge backward and forward with each stroke. Keep your forearms and fingers from cramping by relaxing the return hand and stretching the fingers out straight after every few strokes.

8. Keep your head still and facing forward to maintain a straight course. This also helps with balance.

9. To improve technique, use a wing paddle, which is stronger, lighter and at least 20 per cent more efficient than a conventional flat blade if used properly. It feels slower in the water, forcing you to use good technique. It is best suited to aerated and turbulent water, such as ocean and river paddling, but hard to use for a draw stroke. It is more expensive.

10. Gain paddle fitness by mixing long paddle sessions with intervals and technique sessions. Build distance in long paddles to be at least as long as the kayak legs in your target race. Interval sessions should be as many sets of one to five minutes as you can maintain at your highest capacity. Aim for an accumulated interval time of 15 per cent of total weekly time on the water. If you are doing four hours of paddle training a week, spend about 40 minutes doing intervals, e.g. 10 sets of four minutes. Rough water sessions are good for balance training.

Ian Adamson, Team Nike ACG / Balance Bar

4. Mountaineering

Welcome to the high-altitude world of calculated risk or, as Alpine mountaineer Reinhold Messner put it when describing the climbing game, 'controlling risk'. Your adventure race might not necessarily route you along a 7000m (23,000ft) traverse with technical climbs, but you can bet on being dispatched into the thin-air zone during at least some of the big-name events taking place around the globe. Even though most of your mountain time will be spent on off-road slogging, you would definitely benefit from brushing up on a range of mountaineering skills.

The most basic of these is scrambling, which might encompass anything from a fairly steep hill trek to an on-all-fours scramble along a scree slope. It is a great way to gain elevation fast and to create straight-line shortcut opportunities. However, beware of treacherous terrain, rapidly changing weather conditions and the full gamut of dangers associated with mountain exposure. Remember, too, that high-altitude racing often goes hand in hand with sub-zero temperatures, with snow and sections of ice adding to the challenge.

When traversing snow and ice, a high level of on-the-ground skill is required, so training and certification is a must. Stick with a competent mountaineer until you are experienced enough to assess a mountain environment and confidently maintain a constant forward progression through the obstacles it poses. (See the section on winter disciplines on pages 70–72 for more specific detail about snow and ice disciplines.) Do not take chances; poor judgement can quickly lead to injury or, at worst, a fatal accident. It is also important to keep in mind that high-altitude environments, despite their harshness and apparent desolation, are extremely eco-sensitive and prone to pollution and damage.

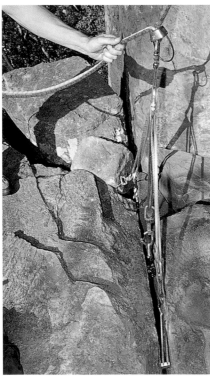

Skills

Mountaineering within the AR context does not require skills overkill and you would do well to stick to the basics. Focus on the following and you will be fine for the majority of AR events: rappelling or abseiling (descending), jumaring (ascending) and traverses (probably an aerial slide or Tyrolean). None of these should be attempted without the requisite experience or equipment, and it would be wise to acquire certification before attempting them during a race.

A weekend skills clinic will teach you how to select and care for rope, the range of knots you will be required to tie, the right way to set up a belay and, most importantly, how to assess your team's safety while racing in the mountains. The activities are reasonably easy to master if you have a good head for heights and sound co-ordination.

When rappelling (racers in many parts of the world may refer to this as abseiling), you will be attached to a fixed rope in order to descend a cliff, often while being belayed, or anchored, on a safety rope (see photographs, left). While comfortably suspended in your harness, you will be clipped via a locking carabiner to a friction device – usually referred to as a Figure 8 – that you use to control your rate of descent.

Ascending (jumaring) requires a bit more practice and co-ordination, using an ascender (Petzl's Grigri or Tibloc are probably the best known of these devices, often referred to as 'jugs' or jumars by climbers). You grip the ascender and slide upward as you progress , allowing it to latch onto the rope as soon as you apply downward pressure

(i.e. your weight) onto it. A second ascender is attached to your harness and nylon webbing loops, into which you slip your feet to effectively 'pump' your way up the rope using leg power.

Finally, chances are you will have to cope with some kind of traverse, whether it is a gravity slide along a zip wire, a fixed-rope via ferrata or a Tyrolean traverse. Zip wires, or flying foxes, require you to take a leap of faith in order to go with gravity along an aerial cable slide, with your momentum usually arrested by water; wear a wetsuit or try to slow yourself down by dragging your feet across the surface.

A via ferrata constitutes a fixed-rope setup along a cliff – or sometimes through a section of fast-flowing river – where racers clip into the in situ ropes and gingerly negotiate the route using their hands and feet.

Tyrolean traverses (imagine yourself clipped via locking carabiners – or friction devices in the case of a steep angle – to a section of rope spanning a crevasse or canyon) come in any combination of distances and angles. It should be easy if the trajectory is reasonably flat, but expect to put in some hard work as soon as the angle of the traverse increases.

As in any AR activity requiring a certain level of skill, practice will make perfect when it comes to mountaineering disciplines, but remember that safety is paramount. Always check and recheck anchors, equipment and attachment points, whether or not the setup has been done by a professional outfit; it might cost you a few minutes of race time, but could save your life.

TOP: **Indirect belays place the body of the belayer into the belay chain, which puts less stress on the anchors, but makes it difficult to escape the system if you need to.**
ABOVE LEFT: **Direct belays place no load on the belayer but need very sturdy anchors.**

10 abseiling safety tips

1. Always use approved gear that has been tested for a specific application.

2. If it is a first-time abseil on an unexplored site, make sure that you do your homework on access and exit points.

3. Always use a safety/belay rope and have at least three separate anchors.

4. It is imperative to have an experienced and qualified person to oversee the abseil.

5. Tie a knot in the bottom of the rope, or else you might fly off the end!

6. Loose pebbles and rocks pose extreme danger; clean the abseil route as best you can before anyone descends to avoid rocks being kicked loose.

7. Always wear an approved, well-fitting helmet and make sure that the chinstrap is securely fastened.

8. Have edge protection (a rope cover, bag or even a backpack) in place so that the rope does not chafe or rub against a sharp edge or point.

9. Check everything before you step off the edge: is your harness on properly, are all carabiners locked, is the friction device connected and is your helmet securely fastened?

10. Avoid loose clothing, extra slings or any item that might get caught in the friction device.

Trevor Ball, Team Energy,
South Africa; owner of Abseil Africa

ABOVE: Stepping over the edge is often the most difficult part of an abseil. Once you get the hang of it, it will feel just like walking backwards off the mountain. Wear a helmet, as your biggest danger is from loose rocks or stones dislodged during your descent.

Equipment

Although race organizers usually supply the majority of mountaineering equipment, expect to see a list of mandatory equipment specified for advanced climbing legs. This could include items such as dynamic rope (contemporary design focuses on an abrasion-resistant, kernmantel construction featuring a core of elastic polyamide fibres protected by a tightly woven sheath), an approved climbing helmet (bicycle helmets are not impact-resistant enough), harness (not too snug that your fingers will not fit between harness and body), prussik loops, carabiners, friction devices and the like (see below).

The extreme environment within which climbing takes place will compel you to think beyond *de facto* climbing gear only; expect to include items such as four-season tents, high-altitude stoves and sub-zero sleeping bags in your pack once you step into the alpine zone. Never cut corners, and thoroughly familiarize yourself with the operating procedures of gear items before you set off on the race rather than waiting until you are at the mercy of a mountain blizzard.

Clothing

When the going gets tough – and it usually does as soon as you hit high ground – you need to have 100 per cent faith in your clothing and gear. As you ascend, the temperature drops, necessitating rugged, thermodynamic clothing and technically advanced, waterproof footwear able to handle anything from scree-slope scrambling to rappelling down the face of a slippery waterfall.

Stick to your layering system, but opt for full-limb, thermal base layer garments. In some cases, you may even need to add an additional mid-layer. Outer layer garments must be rugged enough to cope with abrasive rock and ice, and scuff patches on the knees and elbows will stand you in good stead. Make sure your clothing's cut and design allow ample freedom of movement; where possible, choose jackets and trousers with either articulated knees and elbows or with stretch panels incorporated into these areas. Wind- and waterproof gloves, thermal socks, beanies, neck warmers and scarves, snow gaiters and high-glare eyewear should be considered.

carbiner with
screwgate lock

carbon-fibre
climbing helmet

dynamic rope

figure-8 friction
device

tube friction device

ABOVE: **Mountaineering disciplines are very gear-intensive and you will usually have an assortment of carabiners and friction devices attached to your harness (top right). Dynamic ropes are also standard kit, but may be supplied by the race organizers.**

climbing helmet

AR backpack

wrist-top computer

screwgate carabiner
harness
compass

protective leggings

well-ventilated socks

AR shoes

ABOVE: **Always make sure that you double-check all ropes, anchors and devices before you step over the edge. Your harness should be snug and the chinstrap on your helmet should be well secured.**

5. Winter disciplines

When traversing snow and ice, even basic skills such as walking need to be relearned. Glissading (whizzing down a snow slope on your feet or bum), ice climbing, walking with crampons, using ice axes, ascending steep terrain by kicking steps, digging snow holes for shelter . . . these are but a few of the skills you must master before facing the great whiteout. Beyond the need to acclimatize to higher altitudes and the increased physical energy requirements, route finding in terrain blanketed by snow will become increasingly difficult, while avalanches, ice falls, hidden crevasses and extreme temperatures pose additional dangers. Hypothermia, frostbite and related sub-zero afflictions may easily morph into life-threatening situations; the cardinal rule is to assimilate the necessary experience before putting your life on the line.

For this section, we asked Canadian cross-country ski champion and top adventure racer, Chad Ulansky, currently racing with Team Salomon Canada, about a range of skills, as well as a selection of gear items to improve your chances of surviving the big chill. Here is his advice.

Cross-country skiing

What skis should you use in an adventure race?
There is no simple answer to this question. The skis of choice will depend on snow conditions, terrain and your ability level. Skating skis are fast if the trail is appropriately groomed and you know how to skate. However, most adventure racing will not involve wide, groomed trails. For gently rolling to undulating terrain and packed trails, classic racing skis work well in experienced hands. For newcomers, a shorter, wider ski with some side-cut will improve handling. In more demanding terrain and conditions your team will probably be happier in alpine touring gear, which would be a better option in mountainous terrain.

ABOVE: Firm snow and summer temperatures make for easy going, allowing Team Subaru (Canada) to negotiate this snow slope in light clothing and trail shoes. Once sub-zero temperatures kick in, technical garments and footwear are required.

Should you use skins, wax or waxless skis?

A team is generally faster if all members have the same equipment. With different equipment you travel at the speed of the person having the greatest difficulties. Skins are great in mountainous terrain where there are steep sustained climbs; they take time to put on and take off, so are not well suited to undulating terrain. Waxed and waxless skis are good in flat to undulating terrain and groomed or firm snow. Waxed skis are generally faster than waxless, but waxing requires experience; it is as much an art as a science. As snow changes with differing temperatures, sun exposure and age, carry a selection of waxes with you. The hassle-free nature of waxless skis could save time in the long run.

What training should you do?

A comprehensive training programme is beyond the scope of this section, but remember that in addition to pure physical fitness your training should include improving your technique and your ability to ski in diverse snow conditions. Making telemark turns in breakable crust with a heavy pack is very different to skating your favourite loop at the local ski area.

Snowshoeing

Why snowshoes?

Snowshoes allow virtually anyone who can walk access to snowy places. They are simple to use – just strap them on and start hiking – and can make the difference between wallowing in the snow going nowhere and efficiently covering tens of kilometres.

What type of snowshoes should you use?

The type is not really as important as the size. The larger the snowshoe, the less you will sink in the snow. A small running snowshoe, while good on packed trails, will be nearly useless in deep, unconsolidated snow. Consider your weight (remember your pack) and expected snow conditions when choosing shoes. A good choice for beginners is one of the MSR Denali models, which are light, easily stackable and inexpensive. They also have the option of modular extensions to add flotation to your snowshoe.

ABOVE: Team Salomon Poland, under the leadership of Magda Laczak, battles through the snow in extremely low temperatures with icy winds during the Raid International Ukatak 2002 in Canada.

Glacier travel

Some of the most spectacular sections of races are on glaciers. For anyone who is unprepared and inexperienced they can be dangerous, but for the seasoned racer with appropriate training they can be the highlight of the race.

What hazards should you watch out for on a glacier?

Crevasses! These come in a variety of shapes and sizes – from a few centimetres to tens of metres wide and a hundred metres deep. Also remember to stay alert, keeping an eye out for potential hazards from above, such as avalanches, cornices and icefalls.

What equipment will you need?

The team must be roped up using at least an 8mm (3in) rope. Each person should have two prussiks, two pulleys and a selection of anchors for rescue purposes. If the ice is exposed or the glacier is sufficiently steep, everyone should wear crampons and use ice axes.

What skills should you practise?

Everyone should know how to self arrest with an ice axe. As a team, practise extracting a person from a crevasse. Although there are some excellent books on the subject, they are no substitute for hands-on practice. Find a crevasse you can walk into, or other suitable location, and give it a go.

ABOVE: Team members should be roped together at 10m (33ft) intervals to allow crevasse rescue without impeding forward motion. Be especially careful to maintain some slack on the rope and to pass on terrain information from the front.

ice axe

Must-have winter gear

Keeping warm is critical to success and, more importantly, survival when racing in winter conditions. Relatively minor mistakes made in temperate climes become compounded when in the cold.

There is more to keeping warm in the wilds than having hi-loft garments. Nutrition and hydration are paramount (see Chapters Nine and Ten). In the cold, you need energy for both locomotion and thermogenesis, or keeping warm. If you run out of energy ('bonk' or 'hit the wall'), your decreased level of activity will diminish the heat generated by working muscles that was keeping you warm. Watch your energy level and eat and drink as necessary. The best way to keep warm is to keep moving. If your team's pace slows, you are in for a long cold slog to the next transition.

Clothing requirements are more extensive when racing in the cold. Clothes should be warm, unrestrictive, light and adaptable. In virtually all conditions, dressing in layers is recommended, as this allows you to warm up or cool down quickly (see the section on layering on pages 37–38). The winter racer's enemy is sweat; it will saturate your clothing and you will get cold when you decrease your activity level. Look for garments that maximize aeration through the use of pit zips, vents and leg zips.

The inner wicking layer should be form-fitting and should not absorb water. Most of these garments are made from polypropylene or polyester, with suitable undergarments manufactured by Patagonia Capilene™, Hind Drylete™ and Helly Hansen Lifa™. Choose a middle insulating layer composed of materials such as down, Primaloft™ or fleece. These are listed in order of decreasing warmth per unit weight. Down clothing is lightest and most compressible, but loses virtually all its insulating abilities when wet from precipitation or perspiration. Fleece is relatively heavy and bulky but retains its warmth when wet. Primaloft™ and similar synthetic fills are a compromise between down and fleece; they are quite light, fairly compressible and retain much of their warmth when wet. Select garments based on quality, weight, required warmth, adaptability and, of course, price.

The outer layer must fend off precipitation and wind. Shell fabrics generally compromise their water resistance with their degree of breathability. In conditions warmer than a few degrees below zero, a combination of wet snow, slush and rain requires a fully waterproof shell, preferably made from a waterproof, breathable fabric such as Gore-Tex™ or a host of similar fabrics. In colder conditions, drier snow will not wet through clothing so the outer layer's primary function is to block the wind while dissipating perspiration away from the body. (Various microfibre garments perfect for the job have been discussed earlier, see pages 36–38.)

Keep your hands, feet and head warm. Hands, feet, ears and nose are the first to succumb to the cold, so ensure you have adequate clothing to cover them up. Using chemical heat pads in your gloves and boots is also recommended in extreme conditions, while gaiters help to keep snow out of your socks and shoes.

One final caution: check each other regularly for any signs of frostbite (see page 124); it is far safer to diagnose it early on.

balaclava and warm gloves

crampons

ice boots

ABOVE: Winter clothing needs to retain your body heat while protecting you from the wet and the wind. Layering is imperative, as is covering up your extremities with gloves, balaclavas and scarves.

balaclava

mid-layer fleece

wind and waterproof
shell jacket

thermal beanie

gloves

thermal longs

waterproof
over-trousers

ABOVE: Jackets and leggings add extra bulk for warmth but should do so without
restricting your movements. Select garments that fit well and are manufactured from
fabrics incorporating dynamic stretch to facilitate ease of movement.

6. Other AR disciplines

Creative race directors are constantly racking their brains to come up with ingenious and exciting new disciplines to spice up their events. There are any number of obvious alternatives – horseback riding, canyoning and open-water swimming – but remember that in adventure racing, anything goes. Consider the culture and traditions of the region in which the race takes place and do not be surprised if you have to sail a traditional dhow, paddle a dug-out *mokoro* (canoe) or drag your teammate along in a *pousse-pousse* cart. Here are some of the lesser-known activities you may encounter.

Canyoning

Depending on where you are from in the world, canyoning may also be referred to as canyoneering, kloofing or gorge-running. In a nutshell, it combines a range of rope and trekking skills such as boulder hopping, wading, scrambling, climbing, negotiating traverses and rappelling. Expect to hike into or through canyons and ravines in ecosystems ranging from mountain streams to arid *arroyos*. Swimming along icy streams, wading through fast-flowing rapids, rappelling down waterfalls, jumping off cliffs into deep pools, scrambling up steep cliffs or bounding from rock to rock are just some of the options on this particular adrenalin menu.

It is bound to be a slippery business, so pack your trekking poles to help you maintain your balance while wading along streambeds, and make sure part of your pack has been completely water-proofed. Also ensure your pack is easy to unclip

ABOVE LEFT: **A slippery abseil along a cascading waterfall is just one way in which race organizers might test your nerve.**
ABOVE RIGHT: **Cliff jumps and pack-rafting add to the excitement of a canyoning leg.**

personal flotation device (PFD)

should you get into difficulty in deep water. Never jump into pools without scouting them first to check for submerged logs or rocks and, if you can, wear a wetsuit to protect you from minor scratches and bumps. Negotiate small rapids by wearing a PFD and floating down in a seated position with your feet forward, using your legs and butt to absorb any impact.

Attempt rope work only if someone on the team has the required experience – and do not forget the rope, slings, carabiners, climbing harness and helmet.

A primary danger will be flash floods so it is imperative to assess the extent of the watershed, check long-term weather forecasts and watch for changes in water levels. Check your map, identify possible escape routes from the canyon and discuss these with your team. Hypothermia is also a real possibility, so keep an extra set of clothing in a dry-bag and carry the requisite cold-weather garments.

trekking pole

Coasteering

This is similar in many ways to canyoning, except that it takes place in a marine environment. Race directors will probably set a route following the coastline, compelling teams to traverse anything from pristine beaches to tempestuous and rocky shores. In addition to dealing with rock hopping, currents and beach trekking, you will need to keep an eye on the action of waves and tides, and to cross estuaries and lagoons.

Constantly varying water levels along the coast are a major risk and need consistent monitoring; check the phases of the moon to predict ebb and spring tides, watch out for waves and be mindful of riptides and currents when passing through estuaries. Stick to the compacted, wet sand along the high-water mark during the beach slogs and, if you are forced to rock hop, keep an eye out for freak waves and time your jumps to coincide with the ebb and flow of the ocean. Estuaries pose a probable risk as

sharks often feed where rivers drain into the sea; if in doubt, cross upstream or arrange a ferry if race rules allow. If you end up in a current, swim at right angles to the direction of flow until you escape its force rather than fighting it.

As in canyoning, non-slip shoes, an extra set of dry clothes and warm clothing or a wetsuit are musts. Pack a knife to cut yourself loose if you get caught in kelp, and wear a PFD when attempting deep-water crossings.

ABOVE RIGHT: Hano and Sonja Otto run along the firm beach sand during the 2001 Desert Challenge. Avoid moist sections, which could wet your shoes, making them heavy, as well as possibly causing blisters.

Open-water swimming

You must be a competent swimmer, not necessarily fast, but with the confidence and endurance to stay afloat and maintain forward progression for at least a kilometre in choppy ocean conditions. Obviously this is only a rule of thumb; find out from the race organizer what a specific swimming leg in an event entails to ensure you can cope.

Learn to swim with and without fins and buy a pair you can use without cramping. Use a safety lanyard so as not to lose the fins if you should accidentally kick them off.

Depending on the conditions, you might want to wear a buoyancy device (PFD or wetsuit) to help you float, but you will have to carry it with you before and after the swim. A dry-bag large enough to stuff your pack into is a good flotation device that will also keep your kit dry, but will slow you down.

Whether it is a lake, river or the sea, always check the water conditions first: is there a current, which way does it pull, are there any noticeable hazards? Never dive in head first; rather wade in if you can. Use the current or flow direction of a river to your advantage by entering the water in a position

TOP: **Keep your gear dry by securing it in waterproof dry-bags.**
ABOVE: **Competitors in the Swedish High Coast 400 use their dry-bags as flotation aids. Note that swimming goggles can protect against both sea water and UV rays.**

where the force will help carry you toward your goal. Once you get going, rhythm and breathing is what it is all about. Keep your core temperature stable by wearing a silicone swimming cap and, in very cold waters, a wetsuit or even a drysuit. Wetsuit gloves and a hood will also keep you warm, while goggles, earplugs and nose plugs are non-negotiable for some people.

Horseback riding and pack animals

If you are faced with an equestrian leg during an adventure race, make sure that you are well versed in basic riding skills, such as properly tacking up the animal, how to mount and dismount a horse, and how to get it to walk, canter and gallop. You will be expected to care for, feed and water the animal for the duration of the leg. Designate this responsibility to a team member who finds it easy to establish rapport with animals and check that team kit includes fodder and all the requisite gear.

Staying in the saddle is usually not a problem, but if you do come off, try to fall away from the horse to avoid being trampled and make sure you get your feet out of the stirrups so you cannot be dragged behind a runaway steed. The same techniques apply to most other beasts of burden (*burros*, donkeys or mules), while camels need to be coaxed into a lying position before you can mount them.

In many race situations, one animal will be designated to each team and you will have to decide who runs and who rides, and for how long. If there is no single weaker/sick member in the team, it may make sense to load heavy gear onto the pack animal, with the athletes setting the pace on the ground. Know how to pack your gear on the horse properly, but always carry core kit on your person; make sure you have everything you need on you to ensure survival should the animal bolt. Ride in long trousers without seams to avoid pinching and chafing and wear your helmet to protect your clever bits.

One last tip is to keep a carrot or an apple handy to tempt the animal to stand still (or move forward) when all else fails.

TOP: **Pack animals have limitations; if unsure of terrain, dismount and lead your steed.**
ABOVE RIGHT: **Camels respond to very specific commands so make sure that you pay attention to instructions from their trainers.**

In-line (speed) skating

This is not a discipline often associated with adventure racing, but you would be surprised how many race directors include speed skating in events where some of the race routes follow tarmac roads. It is a discipline that requires a moderate amount of ability and practice and therefore is not something you can learn while racing. Balance is paramount and protective wear a must: think elbow- and kneepads, body armour and good helmets (a safety-certified cycling helmet should suffice). Expert speed skaters will form a 'human train' on long downhill sections by each locking arms around the waist of the person in front, thus reducing drag and increasing the overall speed of the team.

cycling helmet

TOP RIGHT: Opt for well-fitting in-line skates with four wheels and good ankle support.
ABOVE: In-line skating offers an innovative way for race directors to deal with unavoidable sections of tarmac through urbanized regions.

Traditional craft

Many a surprise discipline might pop up during the course of an event, especially if it is taking place in a far-off, exotic destination. The organizers may add a media-friendly discipline with high visual impact to spice up event coverage and contribute to the 'wow' factor for competitors. Anything goes, from poling 'bilibili' bamboo rafts down a river, as competitors did at the 2002 Eco-Challenge in Fiji, to piloting a dhow along the Madagascar coastline. Paddling dugout canoes, sailing pirogues and building log rafts are just some of the traditionally based activities featured in adventure races around the world so far.

In some cases, the race director may supply the teams with a few basic items (logs, planks, rope, wire and tarpaulin come to mind) and expect them to create their own craft. Think laterally and keep the construction as simple as possible. It is not the team with the most innovative craft that will win, but the one that finishes its task quickly and efficiently in order to get onto the water as soon as possible.

TOP: **During the 2002 Eco-Challenge on Fiji Island, local inhabitants wait next to piles of bamboo, which they use to help competitors build their own rafts.**
RIGHT: **Team Subaru (USA) built a *bilibili* raft to negotiate rivers during the 2002 Eco-Challenge.**

Tactics and strategy

As every **AR event** you do will be unique, you need to prepare yourself psychologically to deal with the unknown. Take the hectic time frame of adventure racing into consideration during this mental preparation. When estimating the duration of specific legs, remember that your projected times may be way out, with factors such as navigational errors, changes in weather and unpredictable terrain influencing your progress. Staying focused, especially when getting lost and wasting valuable time, is extremely difficult, but you must realize that losing your cool will only erode team dynamics and discipline.

Added pressure comes from the fact that you will not be sure where the other teams are, whether your route choice is correct or when that threatening rainstorm will hit. Try to visualize the corresponding stress build-up and then imagine yourself operating on four hours of sleep after two hard days of racing and you might begin to have an inkling of the battle awaiting your team. Coping with the challenge will be easier if you are in peak mental and physical condition.

Arm yourself with information about:

1. The race briefing: listen carefully, take notes and ask questions about bearings, resupply points, cut-off times, etc. ✓
2. Tactical planning: know your race regulations, check level of interaction permitted with local populations, and interact with the media ✓
3. Facing the racing: assign responsibilites, follow the 'hear and see' rule, be ready to take on a dark start, plan sleep stops and evacuation procedures ✓
4. Combining disciplines: how to make route choices, how to orienteer yourself on the ground and how to cope with natural obstacles ✓
5. Transition points (TP) and passport control points (PCs): know where they are, what level of interaction is allowed with marshalls, predict when you are likely to reach them, plan the next leg, and record your departure ✓

Dynamics and synergy within the team will also be tested to the maximum; instead of offering criticism, come up with possible solutions. Above all, aim to remain positive and remember to enjoy the race.

TOP: **Navigational errors or other disagreements, coupled with extreme fatigue, could easily erode team spirit during expedition races.**
INSET: **Pain, sleep deprivation and fatigue all take their toll on your mind and body.**

The race briefing: what to expect

Paying attention to pre-race information bulletins and the actual race briefing limits many nasty little surprises. An on-location briefing usually takes place at the Event Centre the night before the race, with the race director informing competitors about race regulations. Maps (usually topographical and to a scale of 1:50,000) and co-ordinates are given out, together with any corrections or alterations. Any mistakes made here might have a huge impact on your race. It is imperative that all team and support-crew members attend the briefing. It is a good idea to have at least two people taking notes – different interpretations of details may be discussed to avoid confusion later.

Race directors occasionally use this forum to drop subtle hints. Think laterally, but never assume anything as fact without checking. Events are often staged so as to include existing hiking trails, natural points of interest and nature reserves or national parks. Listen for mention of these and check your map for corresponding information. At some events, a full set of maps and co-ordinates will be made available, allowing you to plan much of your route in advance. This depends, however, on the type of event and the vision of the organizers, so do not be surprised if you only receive one map and a set of co-ordinates or even just a compass bearing before you start. Make sure you understand what you have received, and when, where and how additional information will be obtained.

The race director will probably read through the race instructions at the briefing, allowing competitors an opportunity for questions. Query anything that is unclear; for example, are the bearings given compass (magnetic) or protractor (true)? Ask about the availability of water on the ground, whether it is drinkable, and double-check the location of any resupply points. What constitutes essential personal kit, which kit items are compulsory on specific race legs and, very importantly, are there any 'dark zones' during the race? These race legs usually constitute technical whitewater, marine or mountaineering sections, which would be too dangerous to do in the dark, and race organizers will halt racing along these during hours of darkness. Factor this into your race plan, making sure you reach these points before the cut-off times; alternatively, conserve your energy and get some sleep on preceding sections. Ask about added options now – for example, is it permissible to portage your boats during the dark zone instead of paddling down the river? If you wait until you are on the ground, it will be too late to ask questions.

ABOVE: **Make sure that all team and support crew members attend the pre-race briefing, and appoint two people to take notes of what is said. Now is the time to ask questions if anything is unclear; it will save both time and frustration when you are in the field.**

Once you have your maps, plot the route co-ordinates and mark the maps in the sequence you will use them. Remember, your compass indicates Magnetic North (see more about this in Chapter Seven, page 99). If any additional maps for hiking trails, nature reserves or wilderness areas are supplied, trace these in on your topographical maps, noting references to specific maps so you may refer to them for detail when you reach that area. PCs, transitions and waypoints should be numbered in sequence to denote your preferred route and marked clearly; highlighter pens work best.

Fold extra maps and store them in a waterproof bag within easy reach. Carry an extra marker and pen to effect changes in the field if you decide on a different route. Appoint a team member to take responsibility for the race instructions, monitoring them constantly along the route. Carry the co-ordinates together with the race instructions to simplify cross-referencing between these two sets of information.

Tactical planning

Since the meteoric rise of media interest in adventure racing (largely due to Mark Burnett's Eco-Challenge, see page 14), television crews and/or print journalists attend many events. The media contingent will congregate at major decision-making points and 'action stations' along the route in order to capture the excitement. Check for any signs of the TV crew; they need vehicles to transport their heavy equipment to various points and identifying their vehicles or tracks might indicate the way to a checkpoint. The flip side is that the sudden appearance of a camera may be enough of a distraction to make you miss an obvious route indicator; concentrate firstly on your navigation and only then factor in possible reasons for media presence.

Another factor that might affect your race tactics is the lunar cycle in the race region; check the calendar and plan your night-time strategy accordingly. Full moon would supply enough light to hike or bike certain terrain types, but if you are stuck with a sliver moon or clouded sky, attempt technically demanding stages during the daylight hours if possible. Inform yourself of specific evacuation procedures in case of emergencies; do you have a sealed mobile phone or radio, should you send up a flare or, if the race is to be called off because of danger along the route, how will that be communicated to your team out in the wilds?

Finally, check the level of assistance permissible from the local population; are they allowed to supply directions or a guide, can you rent a row boat to cross a river, or may you stop in a village to eat a meal? The only way to get answers to all of these issues is to ask before you set off on the race.

ABOVE: Television crews and photojournalists have become a common sight at adventure races. Interact with them if time permits, as this may create excellent media opportunities for your team's sponsors.

Facing the racing

In a perfect world, you will be part of a team where every individual contributes equally toward the overall effort. It is important to agree unanimously on a leadership structure before the race; if one individual is appointed captain, the rest of the team should respect him or her enough to trust decisions made during the race. By the same token, this individual should be mature enough to ask advice, share responsibility and admit when mistakes are made. Some teams prefer to race without an appointed leader, instead allowing individual members to take charge during specific disciplines or legs within which they personally have more experience.

Whatever your decision, assign various tasks to each member: designate specific individuals to carry various mandatory team gear items for various legs, or the entire race; have at least one, preferably two, members on the team with relevant first-aid qualifications; make sure the race passport (usually a laminated, plastic card which you clip or mark at every passport control point, or PC) is attached to the responsible team member where it is clearly visible and easy to reach; an appointed timekeeper should liaise with the navigator, keeping track of time during the race and constantly updating the navigator on how long the team has been moving or when a cut-off will kick in. This is especially important at night when navigation is demanding and your speed of advance and duration of movement are critical in determining progress along a bearing. Route finding – not to be confused with navigation – is an essential race aspect, and if one member can successfully scout the terrain ahead, it will allow the team to move along without having to search for a suitable route. Maintain visual and aural contact between all

team members at all times. This 'hear and see' rule might vary from race to race, but general interpretation enforces a maximum distance of 100m (110yd) between team members.

'Dark starts' are a favourite ploy of sadistic race directors, allowing them to mess with your sleeping patterns even before the race has started. It will be pitch black, probably cold and difficult to pack – psychologically adding to the anticipation at the starting line. In the ensuing rush into the gloom, ensure your team sticks together and does not blindly follow the teams in front of you. Once you start moving, you will quickly warm up; before long, you will want to shed some of your clothing, so plan ahead and wear only what you need at the start. If you suspect you might need additional gear items later on, have them accessible for quick retrieval by your teammates, thus ensuring fluid forward progression.

Race according to the individual strengths of specific team members, but allow the slowest racer to set the pace. Strong mountain bikers, for example, could assist weaker riders by carrying some of their kit or by pushing or pulling uphill using a tow system

ABOVE: Tension during the build-up to the start of the race may be alleviated by ensuring every team member is assigned specific tasks and duties. Here, Team Maybe X-din of Sweden prepares for the 2002 High Coast 400.

consistency is more important than speed. This support should be extended to team navigators as well. Pack their kit and fill water bottles while they plot the next route section; this will allow you to hit the trail as soon as the route planning is done.

The saying 'make hay while the sun shines' definitely applies to AR, where it is important to use daylight to your advantage. If a dark zone is looming, race as hard as you can to beat the cut-off. However, a technically demanding canyoning or mountain-biking section might pose both danger and demoralization if your team attempts it at night, so take team morale and ability into consideration before proceeding. You might take the same time to do the leg with or without sleep, the difference being that your team will now be well rested and full of energy.

Plan sleep stops strategically, where possible sticking to the day/night cycle to which you are physiologically accustomed. Also try to get some sleep before taking on physically or mentally demanding sections, ensuring you are stronger and more alert. It is important to keep sleep at bay for as long as possible, but you have to get the balance right by checking constantly on the condition of all team members. Regular naps (every 18–24 hours) of approximately an hour will often serve you better than four hours of sleep after three days, but this varies from individual to individual and is best evaluated as the race unfolds. There is little value in attempting to sleep in foul weather without a shelter; rather keep moving until you reach a transition point or conditions improve.

Combining your disciplines

Once you have plotted the co-ordinates for the various checkpoints you must visit during the race, you may be tempted to daydream of straight-line travel options. Big mistake. The reality is that there are various route options from Point A to Point B and a direct line is rarely the best choice. Many factors must be considered, but a thorough examination of your map should allow you to gauge the various

instead of racing ahead and waiting impatiently. This negatively affects team dynamics and can be demoralizing. The same goes for other disciplines; rather than getting irritated, helping out will create a positive mental attitude and improve morale. Always remember, especially during multi-day races, that

ABOVE: **Once you are in the transition, concentrate on and finish one task at a time. More haste will generally mean less speed. Keep the space tidy and help others if you finish your tasks before they finish theirs.**

Girl power

Ah, yes, the thrills, chills and spills of being the 'team chick'. After 10 years of hurting myself in foreign countries with four of my closest friends (i.e. adventure racing), I would not have it any other way. Women in AR have a unique role to play, which is both a blessing and a curse. A blessing in that we have a special, indispensable role, we get to sleep in the middle, we can be a calming force, we are good at looking after the boys when they are hurt, we are always special because we bring the best food, and we can make the boys go first on the scary stuff. A curse in that, for better or worse, our performance is closely scrutinized, and we often have to walk a fine line with fragile egos.

One of the main reasons I love being a woman in AR is that it is one of the only sports where it is a distinct advantage. In expedition-length races, a woman's unique physiology and higher body fat actually allow for better performances in extreme heat or cold, and give her the ability to get *stronger* and faster as the race goes on. Another reason is that AR is an 'equal-opportunity destroyer', offering no special dispensation for gender at the elite level. Once that gun goes off, we are no longer men and women, but humans striving together side by side – something unique in the history of sport, and a concept I think would have a positive effect on the world if we were all willing to embrace it.

Robyn Benincasa, Team Nike ACG / Balance Bar

possibilities. Roads, trails and tracks, natural vegetation and plantations, bodies of water and topography will be graphically depicted; all of these, plus factors such as time of day, visibility and weather, will influence your team's final decision.

Depending on the distance and the type of AR discipline, a good track – even up to double the distance or more – usually gets you there faster than bashing your way through off-trail vegetation. Not only do you expend more energy with the latter option, your chances of getting lost are greatly increased and the slightest navigational error might lose you the race. That said, if team morale is high and you might at least halve your distance in easily navigable terrain, what are you waiting for?

As you move along, constantly orient yourself on the ground according to landmarks featured on the map and regularly consult your compass to ensure you remain on the right bearing. Continually keeping an eye on the sun, moon or stars reinforces the fact that you are moving in the right direction. A good

TOP: **Top adventure racer Robyn Benincasa demonstrates her inimitable style.**
ABOVE RIGHT: **Adventure racing is about decision making, and sometimes you need to get off-road and go bushwhacking to gain advantage over other teams.**

tip is to use shadow navigation while moving forward, consistently maintaining your shadow at a specific angle to your line of attack. If in doubt, stop immediately. Rather spend five minutes orienting yourselves on the map than 30 minutes retracing your steps.

Mother Nature has a way of placing challenges in your way, often at a stage of the race when you feel least equipped to deal with them. Bodies of water pose one such obstacle; lakes, rivers, estuaries . . . all must be approached with caution, and every effort

should be made to keep your kit and map dry. Various types of dry-bags are designed to do just that when correctly closed. Garbage (refuse or bin-liner) bags are a bad choice as they rip easily, leaving you to cope with wet and very heavy gear.

Depending on the distance you must swim and the temperature of the water, it might be worthwhile to carry a wetsuit; some racers even carry a set of flippers to minimize their time in the water during longer swims.

Rivers will force you to deal with more than just wet gear and cold water; depending on their flow and volume, they could pose extreme danger. Although the narrowest point might seem the most obvious crossing, this is also where the flow is fastest

ABOVE LEFT: **It is helpful if teammates share responsibilities at transitions between disciplines. Here, while Jim Mandelli pumps up the inflatable kayak, the rest of Team Subaru (Canada) waterproof their rucksacks.**

Crossing a river mouth poses new hazards, including the tide. Check whether it is incoming or outgoing and plan accordingly. If there seems to be a strong outgoing current, move further inland to avoid being dragged out to sea. Bikes and heavy packs might necessitate negotiations with the local population; rowboats or other ferries should operate in the area and, if race regulations permit, make use of local ferries to cross. If all else fails, wait for the tide to go out or walk around.

Marshes or swamps – or, if you will, bogs, quagmires, muskegs, morasses or vleis – are a different and downright dirty obstacle. Muddy conditions slow you down, high reeds and a lack of visible geographical features make visual navigation difficult, while you have to endure the torment of midges, mosquitoes, stinging flies and a host of irritating insects, not to mention the possibility of alligators, crocodiles and other dangerous reptiles. Consider wearing a head-net to ward off the worst attacks from insects, or opt for industrial-strength repellent. A change of footwear is essential – consider wearing wetsuit booties or amphibian sandals – or at least wash your shoes at the end of the wetland section and change your socks.

Canyons, gorges or ravines also slow your rate of progress, so consider a detour if you are not convinced a straight-line route will get you to the next checkpoint more quickly. (Canyoning technique and gear are covered in more detail in Chapter Five, see pages 76–77.) Remember, when racing within the chilly gloom of a canyon, your body will need more fuel in order to generate energy, so eat well and drink regularly to avoid dehydration. Avoid cliffs and precipices as in most cases teams are not packing the requisite technical equipment to negotiate mountaineering sections. Where rappels, traverses or jumars have been included as part of the course, there is a definite potential for bottlenecking; this is one stage of the race where it is acceptable to go full throttle in order to beat a competing team to the front of the queue. Avoid night climbing where possible.

and it often makes more sense to cross at a wider – and probably shallower – point. Waterproof your pack inside a dry-bag and scout the crossing using a stick or your trekking poles, making sure your pack waistband is unfastened so you can remove it easily if you slip. If you need to swim across, enter upriver from the intended exit point and use your dry-bag for flotation. Tying yourself to a rope might be dangerous as it could snag and pull you under. It would make more sense for a strong swimmer to secure a fixed rope to the other bank along which you may then traverse. Avoid crossing a river at night if you are not 100 per cent sure of safety, as you cannot anticipate the dangers you might face in the dark.

sea bootie

TOP: **If a water crossing is not too deep, link arms and walk across, using your trekking poles to stabilize yourselves. Here, Rob Harsh leads Team No Boundaries (USA) through an icy glacial river during the Arctic Team Challenge 2003.**

Heading off-road with your bike brings with it a whole range of possible problems. Expect to portage or, if you insist on riding, to pick up punctures from thorns, sharp sticks or pointy stones. If your tyres are not sufficiently inflated, 'snake-bite' might be another cause of flats. This happens when your tyre crosses a sharp ridge and is compressed so forcefully that the inner tube is punctured against the ridges of the wheel rim, thus causing two small holes – hence the terminology. Always ensure that you fit tyre liners and fill your tubes with puncture-prevention slime. Check the vegetation and topography on your maps before you venture off-trail and only do so if you are assured of gaining a considerable advantage.

Transition points and passport control points

Transition points (TPs) – also called transition areas (TAs) – and passport control points (PCs) or check-points (CPs) are specific markers, indicated by longitude and latitude co-ordinates, along the race route that all competitors have to attend, usually in a specific sequence. Generally, PCs are checkpoints that teams must visit and record by clipping their passport or signing in with a marshall, although they are sometimes unattended. This creates an attendance record enabling the race director to co-ordinate and overview the race status as it unfolds, with race personnel constantly updating race headquarters regarding the position of individual teams. Points are usually marked with a flag, plastic bunting, a flashing strobe at night or a combination of these. Ask about this at the race briefing, ensuring you know exactly what to look for and how to record your visit. If a PC is indicated as part of a technical activity, expect marshals to be in attendance and look out for signs of them – lights at night, vehicle tracks or some kind of shelter.

Support crew are not allowed at PCs and even accidental contact between them and their team might spell the end of the race. Another common mistake is to send a single member to clip a passport while the rest wait; check whether this will break the 'hear and see' rule and act accordingly. Make sure of

TOP: **Clip your passport as soon as you enter a TP and check procedures with race officials.**
ABOVE LEFT: **Think twice before heading off-road on a biking leg. Portaging will significantly reduce your speed of advance and may negate some of the advantage.**

the level of interaction allowed with marshals at PCs. Are you allowed to quiz them on distance, direction or the position of other teams, or might this lead to disqualification or penalization?

TPs string together the individual disciplines making up a multi-sport race. Here, with the exception of unsupported races, chances are high that you will at last reconnect with your support crew. Expect the location to have vehicular access and bargain on electricity and water being part of the deal – especially if the TP also doubles as race headquarters. Keep this in mind when you are navigating your way towards a TP – powerlines and access roads may provide excellent handrails to guide you toward your destination. Once you get there, you will have an opportunity to withdraw for a few precious minutes from the rigours of racing while refuelling your body, attending to medical conditions, replacing gear or catching up on much-needed sleep. In the chaos of getting to a TP, it might slip your mind to sign in with the designated race official; do this as soon as you arrive and also remember to sign out and record your departure. Many tactical decisions revolve around transition points, but beware the lure of support crew comforts: analyze the needs of your team, eat and sleep only as long as you have to, then move on again. Remember, the race clock is ticking.

> **TIP**
> *When you get to a TP after any discipline, wipe your feet with a towel before you put dry socks on. It removes moisture as well as debris.*

ABOVE: Transitions offer team members the opportunity to meet up with their support crew, replenish their water and rations, change their clothes and catch up on some much needed sleep.

Transition and checkpoint tactics begin long before you physically reach them and it is a good idea to indicate the various disciplines between PCs and TPs on your map. This allows you to plan your strategy and gear as you approach the TP, ensuring

that everyone is primed for action when you get there. Apportion a realistic period to be spent in the transition; depending on the state of the race and your position in the field, you might decide to move through at pace, grabbing your gear and food from your support crew and eating on your way out. If you need gear maintenance, morale is low or someone has a niggling injury, rather take time out, interact with your seconds, get some rest and take in some hot food – it is unbelievable what a difference a 20-minute break can make to team spirit.

As in every other facet of adventure racing, teamwork is of the utmost importance and every team and support-crew member should be fully briefed as to his or her responsibilities upon entering a PC or TP. Apportion responsibilities regarding cooking, eating, sleeping, packing, navigation and medical, ensuring you support members of the team who have specific responsibilities. For example, make sure somebody prepares food and gear for the next leg for the navigator while he or she is busy plotting

ABOVE: **Checkpoints may be manned by marshalls and thus very visible (top) or could literally be a tag or clippers attached to an underwater buoy (above left). Double-check procedure with marshalls if they are present.**

Transition tips

- When you enter a TP, find the marshall and make sure he or she records your arrival. If the TP is unmanned, record your arrival according to the race rules (the same goes for a PC).
- Confirm with your teammates and support crew what the next leg will be.
- Drink lots of liquid and eat. Then drink more.
- Ask the support crew if they have any other information that may be useful to the team for the next leg.
- If maps need to be plotted, do that now and plan the next leg of the route.
- Read out a check list of what is required on the next leg.
- Thank your support crew.
- Tell the designated race marshall when you leave, or record your departure in the appropriate manner.

Ugene Nel, Team Energy, South Africa

the next stage. Multi-tasking is the primary key to moving effectively through a transition; think on your feet, communicate clearly and act decisively so as not to waste valuable time.

Support-crew members with the requisite knowledge of map reading and terrain assessment are worth their weight in gold; ask them to scout the best exits from transition points and brief you on the general topography unfolding along the bearing you will be following from the TP. Also discuss your exact strategy as you approach a PC or TP, making sure everyone knows exactly what is required of him or her. This will give all team and support crew members time to mentally prepare themselves. (For more information about involving your support crew in strategy and tactics, *see* Chapter Eight.)

TOP: **Depending on team morale and progress, you could decide to take a breather in a transition, or you may prefer to grab your provisions and eat on the move.**

ABOVE RIGHT: **Your support crew should have scouted the best exit from the transition.**

Navigation

IN **ADVENTURE RACING**, speed is certainly important – but it is worthless if you are heading in the wrong direction.

Navigation is an essential skill enabling you to determine your current position, plot the location of your destination and assess the best route between these two points. A competent navigator should be able to plot grid references (co-ordinates), read map symbols, understand scales, calculate distances and interpret contour lines. Making educated assumptions based on the terrain and map accuracy is also part of a navigator's responsibility, as is orientating a map visually and by compass, following a magnetic bearing – navigating around obstacles where necessary – and selecting a suitable route so that he or she can confidently lead the team from start to finish via checkpoints and transitions.

Fundamentals of map reading

In reality the earth is a 3D sphere. A topographical map is a representation of the earth, drawn to scale, on a sheet of paper. Specific colours, lines and symbols indicate natural features, man-made features and relief.

As a navigator, you should know how to:

1   Plot grid references (co-ordinates) ✓
2   Read map symbols, understand scales and calculate distances ✓
3   Interpret contour lines, assessing slope gradient and determining altitude ✓
4   Make educated assumptions based on the terrain and map accuracy ✓
5   Orientate a map visually and by compass ✓
6   Follow a magnetic bearing, navigating around obstacles where necessary ✓
7   Select a suitable route and confidently lead the team from start to finish via checkpoints and transitions ✓
8   Use navigational techniques such as attack points to confirm your location ✓
9   Take calculated risks to advance your team's standing in the race ✓

Co-ordinates

For convenience, longitude (vertical lines connecting the North and South Poles) and latitude (horizontal lines parallel to the equator) are superimposed on the earth, creating an imaginary grid. The latitude of a location refers to its

TOP: Although most navigational decisions are made by the navigator, it is essential that the whole team is informed and supportive.
INSET: Always make certain that you know exactly where you are on the map.

Useful map symbols and information

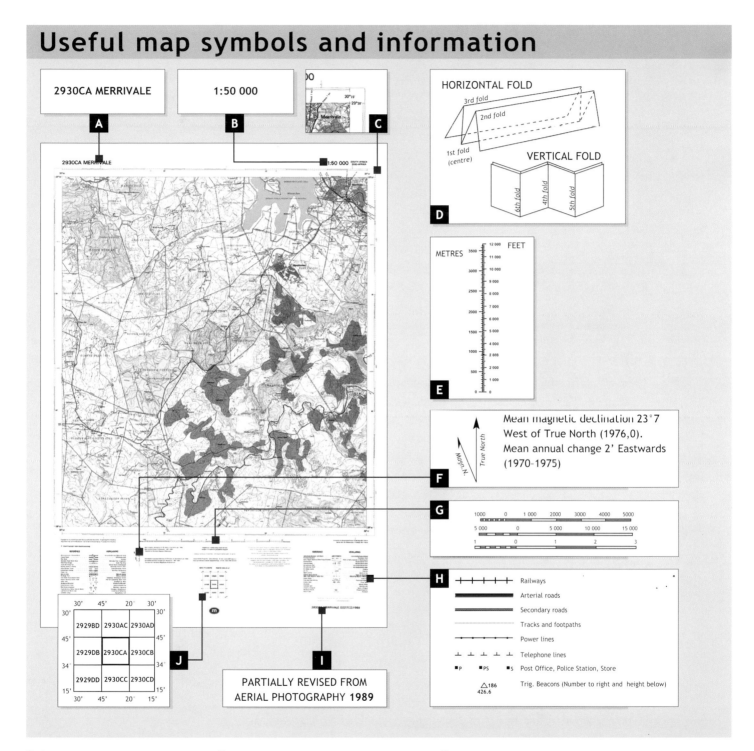

A. Map name and unique number. B. Scale showing ratio in cm/m or in/ft. C. Minutes and degrees East/West and North/South.
D. The correct (and easiest) way to fold a large map. E. Conversion table for metric/imperial distances. F. Magnetic declination
(difference in degrees between True and Magnetic north). G. Distance scale (m/ft; km/miles). H. Legend/key to symbols indicating
natural or man-made structures. I. Date of printing or last revision. J. The position of this map in relation to others in a series.

ABOVE: **On receiving your maps, check the map name, number, scale, date, declination and
the co-ordinate system used before plotting your points. If you have multiple maps, lay
them out on the ground in relation to each other, numbering each one.**

position North or South of the equator, while longitude refers to its position East or West of the Greenwich Meridian, an imaginary vertical line drawn through Greenwich, London.

Thus, latitude/longitude co-ordinates express the precise location of any point on the earth, relative to the lines of longitude and latitude, in degrees, minutes and seconds. One degree is divided into 60 minutes, and one minute into 60 seconds. The form of latitude/longitude co-ordinates is 26°11'16" S and 28°07'12" E.

The Universal Transverse Mercator (UTM) grid divides the earth into 60 zones, excluding the polar regions above 84° North and below 80° South, which use the Universal Polar Stereographic (UPS) grid system. Each UTM zone is 6° wide in longitude and 8° in latitude. The zone blocks are numbered from 1 to 60, starting on the International Date Line (180° longitude) and proceeding East. The zones are 'peeled' off the globe and flattened, introducing distortion. UTM co-ordinates are therefore 'false co-ordinates'. As the UTM grid is based on metres, each degree grid line within a zone is always 1000m wide.

The form of a UTM co-ordinate is 'easting', then 'northing'. The first two digits of a six-digit UTM co-ordinate give the easting (longitude) position, while the third number gives the distance in 100m intervals from the longitude line. The second three digits give the northing (latitude) position and distance. For example: 474 649 tells us that this point is to be found 400m East of the 47° line of longitude and 900m North of the 64° line of latitude.

The Ordnance Survey British Grid (OSBG) covers Great Britain in 100km x 100km square sections, presented in the easting and northing form.

On receiving maps, you should first determine the co-ordinate grid system. Plot each checkpoint and transition, double-checking and labelling each one as you progress. Draw a circle around the point so you do not obscure the detail near the site. Number your maps in relation to each other. Only then assess your route options between each point.

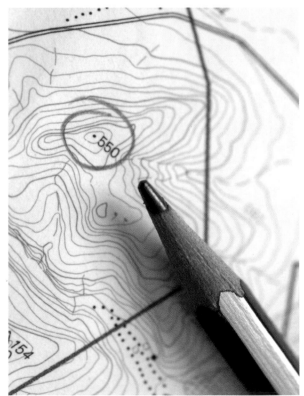

TOP: **Stop to consult your map if there is any doubt that you are on the right track.**
ABOVE RIGHT: **When plotting co-ordinates, draw a neat circle around the point, with your target in the centre. This ensures details surrounding the feature are not obscured.**

Aerial photograph of rugged terrain showing ridges, valleys and rivers. *See* below for how this looks on a map. (Both images reproduced under Government Printer's Copyright Authority No. 11169, dated 26 November 2003.)

Scale

The scale of a map, usually printed at the bottom of the map, expresses the relationship between distance measured on the map and the distance on the ground as a ratio. A 1:50,000 scale indicates that one unit of measurement on the map represents 50,000 units on the ground. Therefore, 1cm on the map represents 50,000cm (500m) on the ground. Scales differ greatly, so note the scale of each map that you receive.

The distance between two points can be measured by an electronic distance measurer, a ruler, a piece of string or even your thumb. 'Calibrate' your thumb on a ruler, noting where the width of your thumb is approximately 2cm. On a 1:50,000 map, one thumb width would then represent 2km on the ground. Calculate and write the distances between waypoints and checkpoints on your map for later reference.

Corresponding map to the photograph above, showing contours and other mapping symbols

ABOVE RIGHT: Envisaging the lines and symbols of a topographical map as real 3D features takes practice. With experience, you will learn to assess the terrain and gradient accurately, choose the best routes and orientate your map with surrounding mountains, rivers and valleys.

Symbols

A legend at the bottom of the map or in the margin provides a reference to the many lines, dots and pictures that are used to represent both natural and man-made features. Symbols are colour-coded in order to make them easy to distinguish.

- **Black:** Man-made features – buildings, fences, tracks, power lines, excavations and railway tracks.
- **Green:** Vegetation – forests, orchards and cultivated lands. Also firebreaks and boundaries of parks and nature reserves. Darker shading indicates more dense vegetation.
- **Blue:** Water features – rivers, lakes and marsh.
- **Brown:** Topographical features – rocky outcrops, sand and erosion. Relief features, i.e. mountains, valleys and cliffs are represented by brown contour lines (discussed below).
- **Purple:** Map revisions.
- **White:** Cleared, runnable land. Roads have their own colours (red, blue and brown) but are outlined in black to indicate that they are man-made. As a general rule, continuous lines indicate permanent features while broken lines depict temporary or less distinguishable features, for instance, a footpath or non-perennial river.

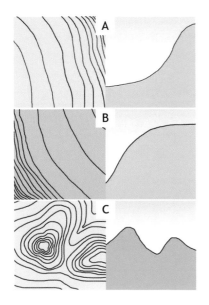

Contour lines

Contour lines are brown, continuous, irregular-shaped circles that join areas of the same height. The resulting patterns represent relief features like hills, valleys, saddles and ridges. With practice, you can learn to interpret the patterns, visualizing the terrain in 3D – a useful tool for establishing your position by observing and identifying features *en route* to your destination.

The height difference between each line is the contour interval and will be indicated at the bottom of the map, or in the margin. On a 1:50,000 map the interval is most often 20m. Be aware when interpreting contour patterns that within the 20m interval there could be a cliff face that is impossible to climb or descend.

- Where altitude is written on the contour line, the bottom of the number will always face downhill.
- The height of a point above sea level can be estimated from the contour lines surrounding it. This reading is the altitude.
- U-shaped patterns indicate valleys or spurs of gentle gradient.
- V-shaped patterns indicate a steep ridge or valley.
- Rivers flow downhill, thus the U or V pattern of a river valley points upstream.
- A spur or ridge is an area of high ground between low-lying areas, or valleys. A saddle is a low-lying area between two higher areas.

The gradient of a slope refers to the vertical height (altitude) gained over a horizontal distance, a factor that influences distance estimation. In a mountainous region, the actual distance covered will be significantly greater than that measured on the flat surface of your map. Contour lines drawn close together indicate that over a short distance, the feature gains or loses altitude. The flattest, easiest route will be one that crosses the fewest contour lines over a greater distance. This route will not only be faster, but easier on your joints when descending and less physically demanding when ascending.

If you have an altimeter, use it as a tool to confirm or establish your position by checking altitude against the contour height on the map. As altimeters work off barometric pressure and are affected by weather systems, reset them regularly at points where you are certain of your position (checkpoint, trig beacon, mountain top), reading your current altitude off the map.

ABOVE LEFT: **These illustrations show examples of contour lines and the features they represent: A. Concave or very steep slope; B. Convex slope; C. Two summits or a saddle with a low-lying area between two ridges.**

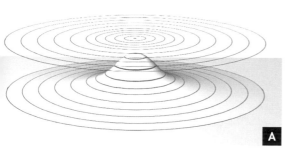

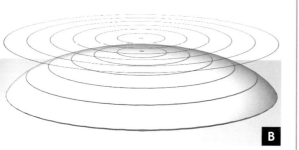

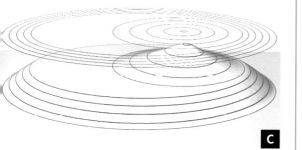

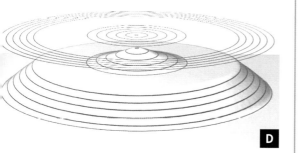

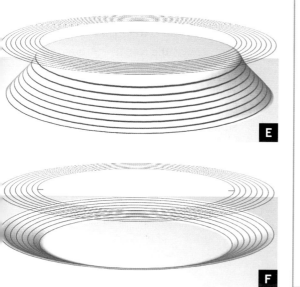

Dealing with magnetic deviation

One of the biggest challenges for adventure athletes is wilderness navigation, and something that trips up many is dealing efficiently with compass deviation (or declination). There are many ways to do this, but only one truly simplifies the task. Rather than performing mental arithmetic or adjusting your compass to correct for deviation, simply draw your own magnetic North line on each map.

Magnetic deviation is the difference between True North, which is what the map is drawn to, and Magnetic North, which is the direction the compass points to. True and Magnetic North are only the same in a few places on earth; everywhere else they vary one way or the other (East or West) by up to 60° in temperate latitudes.

By drawing Magnetic North lines on your map, you reduce the deviation to zero, so you need make no adjustment on your compass or in your head. Here is how to draw the lines on your map:

1. Find the deviation on your map, written in the map key and shown as a symbol in the map border. The symbol shows you which way Magnetic North points (East or West), so make sure the lines you draw point in the same direction.

2. Using your compass (or a protractor) and a 1m ruler, draw two or three evenly spaced lines completely across the map at the deviation angle (shown in degrees).

- A compass can be used like a protractor by rotating the bezel until the angle in degrees lines up with the North index mark on the top of the compass, immediately adjacent to the bezel.
- Place the compass with the lines on the back of the bezel parallel to the side of the map, most easily done by placing it on top of the map border. The body of the compass will now be at an angle to the map.
- Place the ruler along the side of the compass and draw in the Magnetic North line.

Ian Adamson,
Team Nike ACG / Balance Bar

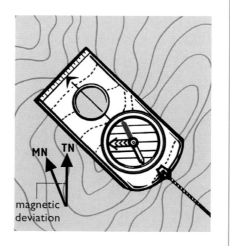

A. Concave slope (contours come closer together near the top); B. Convex (contours move further apart near the top); C. Terrace (flat shelf on hillside); D. Variable slope; E. Steep, constant slope; F. Depression (if a closed contour has tags on the inside, the ground inside is lower than that outside).

Map accuracy

On receiving your maps, immediately check the map date, often printed at the bottom. Some maps may be fairly recent, others more than 25 years old and changes would have taken place. Man-made features are the least reliable. Settlements grow and paths disappear or become roads. Vegetation features are also unreliable; this is because forests may expand and contract while previously cultivated land may become urbanized. Topographical features, such as rivers, hills and valleys, are less likely to change in our lifetimes. If you are unable to recognize a feature represented on the map in your surroundings, then you are not where you think you are.

The compass

A compass is an essential navigational tool used to ascertain direction, but beneficial only if the person wielding it possesses certain skills. The standard compass consists of a base plate and fluid-filled housing, which encapsulates a needle. A direction-of-travel arrow is printed on the base plate. On the housing, a ring of graduations, usually at 2° intervals, marks the 360° of a circle. North is indicated at 0°/360°, South at 180° with East and West at 90° and 270° respectively. On the base of the housing, a number of lines are printed, parallel to North on the dial. An index line underneath the graduated dial is fixed, aligned with the direction-of-travel arrow.

compass

Inside the compass housing, the needle swings freely, stopping once aligned to the earth's magnetic field. The fluid serves to dampen the motion of the needle, allowing it to settle quickly.

The one tip of the needle, coloured red or luminous, always points to magnetic North. In all the following descriptions, this is the side of the needle that must be aligned to North on the dial.

The magnetic field that attracts the compass needle points into the earth at the poles, not along the surface. To prevent the needle from dragging on the base of the housing, resulting in an inaccurate reading, the needle is counter-weighted. Countries are zoned according to magnetic pull. Balanced compasses are available for each of the five zones.

Orientate your map with your compass

It is important to align your map with Magnetic North, so that the direction in which you are travelling and the direction the map is facing are matched, even if this means you are holding the map upside down. Setting your map with your compass helps to associate visible topographic features surrounding you with those represented on the map.

- Place your map on a flat surface.
- Place your compass on the map, aligning the parallel North-South lines on the base of the housing with the Magnetic North line drawn on your map (see 'Dealing with magnetic deviation, on page 99).
- Rotate the map, on which your compass is lying, until the needle is aligned with North on the dial.
- Your map is orientated to Magnetic North.

Bearing

A true bearing is the angle between True North and a specific point measured from a given position. For practical purposes we will only consider magnetic bearings, the angle between Magnetic North and a specific point measured from a given position.

ABOVE RIGHT: **If you take care to align your map with Magnetic North this will make sure that your map faces the direction in which you are going to travel. It also ensures that the map is orientated to the surroundings.**

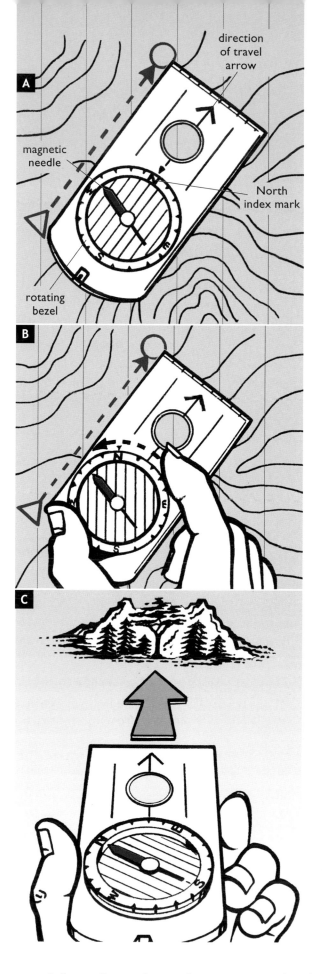

Following a bearing taken off your map from your current position to your destination or a specific feature is a vital skill, especially when no distinct features are visible (flat area, desert, forest), or at night or in fog/blizzard conditions.

Taking a bearing
- Align your map with your compass.
- Draw a line on your map, in pencil, from your current position to your destination.
- Position the centre of the housing over your current position with the direction-of-travel arrow pointing toward your destination.
- Turn the housing until the needle is aligned with North on the dial.
- The bearing is the angle indicated by the index line.
- Also note the back bearing – the angle on the opposite side of the compass (bearing minus 180°). This is usually used when retracing your steps or as a reference point when the feature you have left is distinctive.

A sighting compass enables you to take an accurate bearing from your current position to a feature by looking at the feature and reading the bearing off the dial. This technique is less accurate when you are using a hand-held base-plate compass.

Walking on a bearing
- Take a bearing from your map or, if given a bearing, turn the housing so that the index line is set on the given angle.
- Hold your compass level.
- Face the same direction as your direction-of-travel arrow. Align the needle with North on the dial by turning your body.
- Look at the features directly in front of you and select one, such as a tree or rock, which is about 100m away.
- Walk to the feature and select another feature ahead, again using your compass to confirm your direction.

ABOVE: **A. Draw a line on the map from your current location to your destination; align the direction-of-travel arrow; B. Turn the needle housing so North on the dial is aligned to the compass needle; C. Walk in the direction shown by the direction-of-travel arrow, keeping the compass needle on North.**

To walk on a bearing, move in the direction of your direction-of-travel arrow, keeping the compass needle aligned to North on the dial. Choose way-points (discussed below) at regular intervals, minimizing the margin of error that results if you deviate from the bearing. Accurately following a bearing comes with practice. A 6° deviation over 500m will land you 52m away from your target. Over greater distances you will end up further off-course. It is far easier to walk toward a feature than to keep your eyes focused only on your compass.

Magnetic deviation, or error, often results when the needle is affected by other magnetic forces produced by metal, rocks and ore deposits, electrical appliances, power lines, railways tracks and cars.

Global positioning system (GPS)

A GPS uses signals from satellites orbiting the earth to determine position. GPS co-ordinates are accurate to within 5m of your actual position, but this powerful navigational tool is often banned in adventure races.

A GPS can track your progress, display your altitude, ascent rate, descent rate, straight-line speed and distance covered, and will indicate the direction of your target, by means of an arrow, in relation to your current location, 'as the crow flies'. It does not account for mountains, ravines, rivers, large bodies of water and cliff faces – obstacles you would rather avoid where possible. But, if used in conjunction with a topographical map, you just cannot – or at least should not – get lost.

Sporty GPS wristwatches are also available, but although you cannot key in waypoints and they do not display positional information, they are not allowed at most events. Consider two teams racing against each other along a beach. They both know from the map that the distance to the checkpoint is 9km. The team with the wristwatch can put their heads down and run, stopping right in front of the checkpoint when an alarm on the watch tells them that they have covered 9km. The other team will probably progress more slowly as they are estimating distance from their pace and trying to confirm their position from topographical features such as sand dunes or rocky outcrops.

While a GPS detracts from the challenges of map and compass navigation, it may have a place in AR where permitted. It is useful in the desert, where there are no distinct topographical features, or on the ocean where you are paddling across massive bodies of water, surrounded by nothing but rolling swells. Even if it is kept sealed, only to be used in an emergency, it confers a sense of safety for both competitors and race directors.

Navigation techniques

The ability to orientate your map and follow a compass bearing to arrive at your destination in any weather condition, during day or night, is the essence of navigation in adventure racing. When visibility is good, distinct landmarks affect your direction of travel and confirm your location. When you are unable to identify prominent features due to the nature of the terrain, weather or time of day, your compass is your only guide.

With regular practice and by applying the following techniques, you can minimize navigational errors:
- Walk with your map and *compass in hand*; cycle with your map on a map board.
- *Never take your eyes off your map.* If you know where you are on the map, you are not lost.
- *Correctly identify landmarks* and do not make assumptions. If a mountain ahead of you does not fit the contour pattern of a similarly large feature represented on the map, do not try to make it fit. You are not where you think you are.
- *Attack points* are features such as streams, bridges, settlements, path junctions and mountain peaks on the way to your target, which break your route into smaller sections and bolster your

ABOVE: **GPS devices, though restricted in most adventure races, may have a place when races pass through environments where distinct topographical features are not present, for instance, jungle, sea or desert.**

confidence by confirming your location. Keep the distance between attack points short, correcting early if you travel off-course.

- *Handrails* are long linear features such as rivers, power lines, tracks and fences that may run in the general direction in which you wish to travel. They are easy to follow and make navigation easier but could distract you. At some point you will have to deviate from the handrail in order to reach your destination.

- A *catching feature* is one that lies a little beyond your target. When giving friends directions, you may tell them that they have gone too far if they reach the intersection. This is a catching feature, an indication of when they have overshot the mark. Should you reach a catching point, back-track immediately.

- When trying to *locate a specific point*, such as a hut alongside a river, deliberately aim off. Take a bearing to a point a few hundred metres upstream of the hut. When you reach the river, you will not have to decide whether to head upstream or downstream to find the hut; it will lie downstream from you within a few hundred metres.

- Errors resulting from *inaccurate distance judgement* are common and can be solved by timing and pace counting. In training, time how long it takes you to cover a measured distance up steep slopes, through vegetation and on flat open ground. Count the number of strides taken to cover the same distance. Knowing, for instance, that if the terrain is flat and grassy, it will take you four minutes and 325 strides to cover 500m may be useful during a race.

- When walking on a bearing in *low visibility*, string out your teammates at intervals, within sight and not more than 25m (27yd) apart. While the navigator leads, the back person should set a compass on the bearing, sighting line of travel through intermediate team members to pick up any deviation.

Route options

A well-planned course should offer numerous route options from one checkpoint to another. It is only fair that cunning strategy and selecting navigationally challenging route choices, such as heading straight through a seemingly impenetrable forest, should count in your favour. Taking a risky option may set you back hours, but could also catapult your team ahead of more cautious competitors.

When selecting your route, consider the terrain (slope and vegetation), handrails, attack points and teammates' physical condition, as well as the time of day. If it is night, you are all tired and a teammate is weak, walking an extra 10km (6 miles) on a smooth road is a better choice.

If you receive additional maps (hiking trails, nature reserves), transfer this information on to your topographical map. Only use highlighters to mark your routes, a different colour for each discipline. Fine-liners smudge when wet and thick felt-tip pens obscure detail.

ABOVE: On a course with numerous route options, risky choices may count in your favour and keep you on track as long as you apply sound navigational techniques when you select your route.

Error recovery

While every situation is different, the sooner you realize your error, the easier it is to correct.

- Orientate your map to your compass.
- Try to match features represented on the map with those in your surroundings.
- Do not proceed unless you are certain of your location.
- If necessary, backtrack to your last position of certainty or an identifiable feature.
- If you are tired, sleep.
- If it is night, sleep until morning when daylight will reveal your surroundings.
- Do not argue with your teammates or separate from the rest of the team.
- Do not quit; if you are lost, others are lost too.
- You are only out of the race when the race director pulls you off the course.

The navigator's role

The navigator's role is to lead the team from one point to the next, selecting the best routes. It is a stressful responsibility as decisions he or she makes impact the whole team. The navigator should keep the team informed as to where they are going and what terrain they are to traverse, and should ask for another opinion if undecided. The team should know at all times what decisions are being made. Assigning supportive tasks to each team member helps the navigator, makes team members feel valuable, and keeps the team focused – a factor that greatly contributes to the management of sleep deprivation. Some task assignments are:

- The passport custodian is responsible for punching the passport.
- Two people can count strides to determine distance covered.
- The timekeeper marks the time passed from one waypoint to another to judge distance according to pace.
- When the navigator calls, 'Path on left in 400m,' the feature spotter looks out for it, calling back other features observed.

Even the world's most experienced navigators make mistakes so do not blame yours. Instead, offer help to correct the error. For longer events, a secondary navigator is a good idea.

If you are confident of your navigation abilities, are willing to take risks, and have your team's approval, do so. With experience you will make better decisions and will learn far more from correcting mistakes than by progressing through the course with ease.

ABOVE: **For the navigator, taking a team through a race is a stressful responsibility. This challenging task can, however, be made easier if the navigator is given full support by the rest of the team members.**

Keep detailed information on each team member in a folder. This includes name, age, telephone, address, ID number, blood group, passport details, medical information (medication being taken, allergies, vaccinations, medical aid number), and next-of-kin contact information.

If you are unfamiliar with the support vehicle, drive it before you leave. Practise manoeuvring the trailer and learn how to access the wheels and the spare, change the tyres and use the jack.

Preparing a menu for four individuals is no easy task. With time, you will learn what works best:

- Begin by getting the team together to discuss likes, dislikes, allergies and any other dietary peculiarities. Get their consensus on the important things like proteins (red meat, chicken, fish, vegetable protein, eggs), carbohydrates (white/brown bread, rice, potato, sweet potato, pasta), fruits, vegetables, sandwich fillings (cheese, egg mayo, peanut butter and syrup, tuna mayo), and drinks.

- Plan carefully by going through the stages of the race. You will need dinner for the night before the race, a snack before the race start, snack-pack goodies, one main meal for each day of the race and two extra meals, in case you need them. You also need liquids – water, energy drinks, juice and hot drinks.

- Check whether the water at the start venue is drinkable and whether you can buy water.

- Plan simple meals that can be warmed up in a single pot.

- Write a shopping list of goods and quantities to buy, then go shopping. Buy only what you need.

- Pre-cook and freeze as much as possible at home.

- Keep a dedicated crate as a 'race pantry' for items such as tinfoil, Ziploc™ bags, sandwich spreads, tea, coffee, sugar, salt, pepper, seasonings, condiments, and so forth. Make a check list for your pantry and replenish your supplies after each race so that you do not have to do this in a mad rush before the next event your team enters.

ABOVE: It is the support crew's responsibility to keep the transition area ordered and tidy, with food, water and equipment readily accessible. Each competitor should have a separate area for his or her kit.

- Pack products like sugar, cereal, pasta and rice in sealed plastic containers instead of leaving them in their original packaging. Keep your 'kitchen' tidy and organized.
- Pack coloured tags or sticky nametags to label food packs, especially if dietary preferences of the various team members differ.

Pre-start

This period is both sociable and stressful; as teams await the race briefing, they are not only excited but apprehensive.

- Take notes at the briefing, recording both racer and support instructions.
- Help the competitors to pack their backpacks and crates, confirming and checking off compulsory equipment.
- As you are the one who will be working with the boxes of gear, either watch them being packed or pack them yourself so you know where to find things. Pack related items together, e.g. bicycle spares, cooking equipment.
- Label the outside of each crate, listing the contents.
- The racers should initial each item of their clothing and equipment.
- Load the crates on the vehicle yourself. The things you will need first, such as tarpaulins and race crates, should be packed last.
- As the navigator plans the route, take note of disciplines, distances and transitions. This aids in meal planning and, though unreliable, gives you an idea of when to expect the team.
- Before going to sleep, fill thermos flasks with boiling water and prepare breakfast, sandwiches, fluids and snack packs. Make certain that the racers are ready and that only overnight equipment needs to be packed before the start.

TOP: **A makeshift settlement at the Arctic Team Challenge 2003. The transition area is rarely devoid of activity as teams constantly arrive and depart.**

ABOVE RIGHT: **Hot drinks are always welcome when teams make it to the transitions.**

The race

Now your work really begins.

- Get up before the team, offering them mugs of tea, coffee or hot chocolate and something to eat. Pack the vehicle and make sure that you cheer them off at the start.
- If you have to travel in convoy, be prompt and listen to instructions. If you are travelling independently, ensure you know where you are going before you leave.
- Once you get to the transition area, check in with the transition official. Enquire about new maps or instructions and ask if you can assist your team – for example, by carrying their kayaks out of the water when they arrive or carrying them down to the water.
- Set up camp, rolling out your big tarpaulin first, creating a clean surface on which to set out crates. If necessary, put up your shelter for shade and wind/rain protection.

- Designate a 'racers tarp'. Unload the racers' crates, assigning a corner of the tarpaulin to each team member. Place a chair next to the crate and keep this layout identical at each transition. Racers are creatures of habit and will usually automatically go to their assigned places.
- Prepare sandwiches, snack packs and meals. Wash and dry clothing. Check boats and bicycles. Set out clothing and equipment for the next stage. Toilet paper and medical supplies should be easily accessible. Only once you have completed these chores are you free to eat, sleep and socialize.
- There is no need for you to stay awake for hours on end. Your team needs you to be rested. Take turns sleeping or ask your team to wake you when they arrive. Teams are often hours overdue and since you have everything organized you will not be caught unprepared.
- When other competing teams come in, take notes. Record their names and times of arrival and departure. Also note their condition and

ABOVE: **Team Hexal enjoys a short break during the Africa Adventure Quest 2001. They went on to win the event, which formed part of the Discovery Channel AR World Championships.**

direction of departure. Your team will almost inevitably ask for this information.

• When your team comes in, start your stopwatch, calling out at five-minute intervals. The team captain will tell you how long they are planning to spend. Make sure they leave on time.

• Fill up hydration bladders and replace old food packets with new ones. Do not remove any other gear from their packs.

• Train them to toss wet and dirty gear into a crate you have provided.

• If they are having a meal, hand them bowls and spoons, making sure that they eat.

• As they leave, check their mandatory gear. Wish them well, tell them they are looking great and that you are proud of them. They will appreciate your support and encouragement.

• Once your team has left, pack up quickly. Dishes and wet clothing can be dealt with later when you are waiting for your team at the next transition. Load the crates and strap down boats and bicycles securely.

• Confirm directions to the next transition before leaving. Travelling immediately to the next transition allows you time to deal with flat tyres or even getting lost. You may also want to stop at a shop to replenish supplies.

Useful skills

Navigation

It is certainly worth your while to attend a navigation course, learning how to plot co-ordinates and interpret maps. If you get maps and instructions in the transition area while your team is still out, you can plot the co-ordinates and assess route options, briefing the navigator when the team reaches the transition. Waiting for them, you have time to plot accurately, checking for errors. In the later stages of the race when the navigator is sleep deprived, your assistance will be much appreciated.

Knowing how to navigate will also prevent you from getting lost on the way to a transition.

ABOVE RIGHT: Home away from home, the support crew and transition area cater to the racers' primal desires: food, water, rest and – last, but certainly not least – emotional support.

Therapist

As an assistant on the support crew, you have to cope with your own emotional highs and lows brought about by seeing your team in safely, worrying when they are delayed in worsening conditions, driving while sleep deprived and dealing with situations such as fixing bikes and finding food and water. But, when your team comes into the transition, the team is your priority. Now is the time for you to provide emotional support. You may need to smooth team-dynamic issues or encourage the team to continue. For the most part, knowing that you are waiting for them with a friendly smile and warm food will motivate each member to do his or her best — for themselves, their teammates and you.

First aid

Common afflictions suffered by adventure racers include blisters and associated feet problems, as well as digestive complaints (diarrhoea and vomiting), wounds (cuts and gashes), hypothermia and insect bites. Inflammation and joint, tendon and muscular injuries will crop up regularly. Know how to clean wounds, fix feet, strap joints, as well as how to massage muscles and administer medication to relieve inflammation and digestive ailments.

Mechanics

Read bicycle manuals and ask friends to teach you how to change tyres, fix punctures, replace brake and gear cables, tune gears, repair chains, and what should be lubricated. Depending on the disciplines, you may also need to know how to fix fibreglass boats, rig sails and coil ropes.

Driving 101

A driving course will teach you how to handle wet roads, steep inclines and blowouts. You should also learn how to operate a high-lift jack, change tyres, dry spark plugs and engage 4x4 when necessary. Ensure that you are confident in your ability to cope with any situation — and assist other crews.

Team relationships

Support crews give up their time to assist other people. It is fair that their expenses for transport and accommodation are covered and that food is provided. They should also wear team sweaters, hats and shirts, identifying them as part of the team. As your relationship develops, you may want to add to the crew's apparel.

TOP: **In your role as therapist, you will remedy both emotional and physical ailments.**
ABOVE: **The support crew are essential members of the team. Without their dedication, commitment and assistance, the racers would not even make the race start.**

Should you pay your support crew? It probably depends on the financial status of the team. If your crew has taken unpaid leave from work to assist the team, then some kind of remuneration may be appreciated. I cannot think of any crew who offers their services expecting compensation above having their costs covered. They are involved because they love this sport, care for their team members and reap their rewards from being able to assist.

Support crews present an opportunity to be a part of a team. If you are new to the sport, or hesitant about participating, becoming part of a support crew will give you an insider's view. If you have been injured, you can still be involved. As a racer, you will learn much that will streamline your own racing. Finally, if you are a sponsor, friend or family member, you can show your support by assisting the team.

You get to see to some amazing places, meeting other people who love the outdoors. Although assisting is hard work and many little things you do will go unnoticed, it is a satisfying experience.

ABOVE: Exotic wilderness locations are synonymous with adventure racing events, which present an ideal opportunity to conquer new lands, see spectacular sights and take on terrain that is infrequently visited.

Fuelling your body

THE **CHAPTER DOES NOT** tell you how many calories to consume, nor teach you to compute your protein, carbohydrate and fat intake. Instead, it explains nutrition basics like why proteins, carbohydrates, fats and fibre are important, and suggests you should follow sound nutritional guidelines to discover what works for you during an event. Remember, it is important to eat what you enjoy and can get down – and keep down.

Proteins

1. Proteins are often neglected in favour of carbohydrates, but are vital. During digestion, they are broken down into amino acids, which are involved in almost every biological process from metabolism to the growth, repair and maintenance of cells – including muscle cells – as well as hormone and enzyme production.
2. During prolonged activity, or when the body runs out of carbohydrates, proteins are released from muscle cells for use as energy. This means these amino acids are no longer available for building and maintaining muscle tissue. To ensure a ready supply of amino acids, each snack and meal you eat should

Racers' favourite foods:

Specific foods eaten before an event
None of the racers we spoke to has a specific pre-race programme, but they all eat more and increase their carbohydrate intake.

Snack bags (also for emergency 24hr supplies)
Raisins; peanuts; mixed nuts; chocolate; sandwiches; nut, sesame seed and muesli bars; dried fruit; fruit bars; potato crisps; boiled baby potatoes; biltong (beef jerky); a few carbohydrate bars and sweets (jelly babies and nougat).

Favourite sandwich fillings
Peanut butter and syrup or honey, cheese, jam, Marmite/Bovril, chicken mayo, ham and cheese.

In transition – hot meals
Soup, starch (pasta, rice or baby potatoes) with a sauce (chicken and vegetables, or tuna and tomato sauce)

In transition – quick meals
Oatmeal porridge (in the morning), baby potatoes, bananas and other fruit, banana bread, protein shakes, muffins, sandwiches, hotdogs, soup.

Supplements taken during events
Few racers use carbohydrate-electrolyte gels, more use protein shakes. All of them drink mainly water. Most racers drink fruit juice or a little carbohydrate-electrolyte drink for flavour and variety. Few of them take vitamin and mineral supplements during events.

Post-race cravings
All crave proteins, especially steak, salty foods that are high in fat, fresh fruits and lots of vegetables.

TOP: **Eating frequent snacks will fuel your body for optimal performance.**
INSET: **Almonds and other nuts make perfect on-the-trail snacks. They are high in unsaturated fats, providing more energy than either proteins or carbohydrates.**

contain some protein. As the type of protein is as important as the amount, eat a variety of plant proteins (e.g. nuts, lentils, legumes) and animal proteins (e.g. chicken, tuna, biltong/jerky).

3. Remember, consuming proteins improves your performance and endurance later in the race and speeds your recovery after the event.

4. Protein supplements offer a convenient protein source that can be eaten between or with meals. Shakes are nutritious and taste good, but bars are often unpalatable and hard to get down.

Fats

1. Fats, or lipids, help to regulate temperature, distribute the fat-soluble vitamins A, D, E and K, produce energy, form cell membranes and synthesize steroids/hormones.

2. They improve the palatability of meals.

3. Fats are a concentrated energy source utilized in endurance sports.

4. Eat foods that favour unsaturated fats, which are liquid at room temperature (vegetable and fish oils), rather than saturated fats, which are solid at room temperature (animal fats).

5. Omega-3 and omega-6 essential fatty acids reduce muscle damage and increase recovery rates. They cannot be synthesized in the body and must be supplied by foods containing them (e.g. olive and sunflower oil, linseed, walnuts, sardines, salmon).

Carbohydrates

1. The rate at which carbohydrates, such as sweet foods and starches like rice, potatoes, pasta and bread, are broken down and absorbed depends on the type of sugar (e.g. glucose is absorbed more quickly than fructose) and the complexity of their structure. A monosaccharide (single sugar unit) like glucose does not need to be digested, while polysaccharides (complex carbohydrates made up of numerous sugar units) like starch take a while to be 'disassembled' into single units.

2. Carbohydrates are to your body what petrol or gasoline is to your car – fuel. In the blood, elevated glucose levels stimulate the pancreas to secrete the hormone, insulin, which facilitates the uptake of glucose by your muscle and liver cells. Inside the cells, glucose is used to produce energy, giving off heat as a by-product. Excess glucose is stored in the cells as glycogen – a small but readily available supply.

Carbohydrates listed on food and beverage labels

- *Monosaccharides*: glucose, fructose, sorbitol, galactose, mannitol, mannose.
- *Disaccharides*: sucrose (1 glucose + 1 fructose), maltose (2 glucose) and lactose (1 glucose + 1 galactose).
- *Polysaccharides*: starch, glycogen, dextrin and cellulose are chains of glucose. Maltodextrin is a processed glucose chain, which is shorter than starch and more water-soluble. The carbohydrate, inulin, is made up of multiple fructose molecules.

TOP LEFT: **Protein, often neglected during events, improves performance and endurance.**

TOP RIGHT: **In transition, pasta, rice and potatoes mixed with a sauce make a nutritious meal.**

ABOVE: **Omega-3 and omega-6 essential fatty acids reduce muscle damage and increase recovery rates.**

3. 'Hitting the wall' or 'bonking' happens when blood glucose levels drop rapidly or the body runs out of blood glucose and glycogen. Symptoms of low blood glucose (hypoglycaemia) include weakness, irritability, confusion, fatigue, headaches, sweating and a rapid but weak pulse. Body temperature drops and you may become unconscious. Whatever you eat to remedy this must first be digested to release energy-generating molecules in the form of glucose that can be utilized by your muscle cells. Remember, then, that it will take five to 30 minutes for recovery to begin, depending on the level of glycogen depletion and type of carbohydrate consumed.

4. The Glycaemic Index, or GI (see table on page 117), is a useful indicator of the rate at which carbohydrates are converted into glucose in the bloodstream. High-GI foods affect blood glucose levels almost immediately, while low-GI foods enter the bloodstream at a slow, steady rate to increase performance and delay fatigue. Regularly eat small portions of both high- and low-GI carbohydrates to keep blood sugar and energy levels stable and avoid hypoglycaemia.

Carbohydrate-electrolyte drinks and gels

1. Carbohydrate-electrolyte drinks predominantly contain water, carbohydrates and electrolytes. While replacing fluid is the primary benefit (see dehydration and hyponatraemia on page 125), their value is questionable; there is no definitive evidence showing carbohydrate-electrolyte products enhance performance in excess of the benefits gained from consuming an equal volume of water and a balanced diet. However, during AR events when you sweat excessively and do not eat regularly, they may help to preserve glycogen stores and prevent depletion.

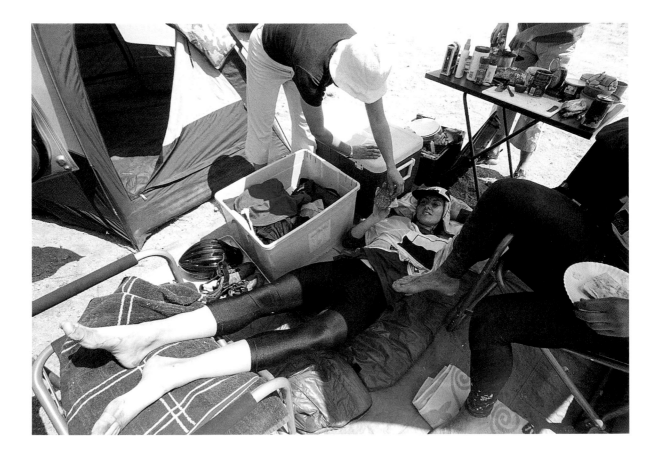

ABOVE: **Recovery after 'hitting the wall' will only begin once the body's depleted supply of blood glucose and glycogen is replenished. This takes from five to 30 minutes, depending on how low glycogen levels are and what type of carbohydrate is consumed.**

Energy drinks

2. Most carbohydrate-electrolyte drinks contain glucose and sucrose, giving them a high GI and sweet taste. Those with more glucose polymers taste less sweet. Choose products with a carbohydrate concentration of less than 10g/100ml (4–8 per cent is ideal). Higher concentrations may make you nauseous.

3. Carbohydrate-electrolyte gels are lightweight carbohydrates conveniently packaged in waterproof sachets. As glucose polymers break down to glucose when exposed to light, packaging should be foil or non-transparent. Each 30g sachet contains up to 12g (40 per cent) carbohydrate and must be consumed with water (at least 100ml/12g carbohydrate). Those containing a higher percentage of carbohydrates should not be consumed at one sitting.

4. Mix-with-water powders are easy to carry, making flavoured drinks that are more palatable than water, encouraging you to drink.

5. Keep water in your hydration system and a carbohydrate-electrolyte drink in your water bottle for variety.

energy squeeze

sports drinks

corn syrup

energy shake

squeezable energy gel

sports drink powder

carbohydrate/ vitamin energy supplement

Glycaemic Index (GI) of common foods

High GI	Medium GI	Low GI
• Bread (white, brown, wholewheat, rye)	• Rice (Basmati, brown, white), couscous	• Soybeans, butter beans, chickpeas, barley, lentils
• Cornflakes, Rice Krispies, Cheerios, CocoPops	• Pasta (most types), gnocchi, instant noodles	• Yoghurt, full-cream milk, soy milk
• Rice cakes, pretzels	• Bran cereal, shredded wheat, muesli, oatmeal porridge	• Apples
• Potato (instant mashed, boiled and mashed), pumpkin	• Muffins, oatmeal cookies	• Tomato soup
• Maltose, glucose, honey	• High fructose corn syrup, sucrose, fruit jams	• Fructose
• Dates	• Raisins, sultanas	• Peanuts, M&M's (peanut)
• Jellybeans	• Bananas, grapes, oranges, mangoes	
	• Baked beans, sweet corn, sweet potatoes	
	• Snickers bar, Mars Bar	
	• Potato crisps, popcorn	
	• Sponge cake, banana bread, fruit loaf	

ABOVE: **Although carbohydrate-electrolyte drinks and gels are not essential, they do help to provide hydration, which is crucial. During a race when you sweat a great deal, they may also assist in preventing your stores of glycogen from becoming depleted.**

Carbohydrate drinks/gels and tooth decay

'Sticky' sugars found in energy drinks and gels adhere to your gums and teeth. They are absorbed through tooth enamel and dentine, penetrating the root canal, where they break down into acids that cause tooth decay from the inside out. By the time cavities appear, decay is extensive. X-rays allow early diagnosis. Sensitivity to cold and sweetness is not an accurate indicator.

To prevent tooth decay, gargle with lukewarm salt water in transition and after events to rinse your mouth, flush stickiness, tone gums and neutralise the acidic pH. Avoid putting carbohydrate drinks in your hydration system. Sipping continuously on these sweet liquids for hours and days aggravates decay.

Carbohydrate bars

1. The same principles apply to carbohydrate bars as to carbohydrate drinks and gels. They are convenient, most are palatable and they pack a large amount of carbohydrate into a relatively lightweight bar.
2. Ideally, bars should contain 30g of carbohydrate in a 50g bar, 5–10g of protein and have a fat content of not more than 5g.
3. Divide the bar into thirds and eat over 20–30min, washing it down with water. Bear in mind that it takes 30–45min for the carbohydrate to be metabolized.

Fibre

1. Fibre cannot be digested in the human gut and provides no energy, but is important to promote sugar absorption into the bloodstream and efficient functioning of your intestines.
2. Fibre in fruits, vegetables, legumes and bran cereals prevents constipation by softening the stool and encouraging normal elimination.
3. Regular bowel movements in multi-day races should not be neglected, so be sure not to neglect your fibre intake.

TOP: **Water bladders are popular hydration systems that fit conveniently into a pouch in your backpack. Keep them for water, and carry carbohydrate-electrolyte solution in a bottle.**

Supplements

Pharmacies have sections devoted to nutritional supplements, each claiming to be the best and offering more than the Recommended Dietary Allowance (RDA) of each scientifically formulated ingredient.

We need vitamins to maintain normal body functioning and to facilitate blood clotting, protein synthesis, metabolism and bone formation. We need minerals to strengthen teeth and bones and help vitamins do their work. For instance, magnesium prevents muscle cramps, while iron deficiency results in anaemia, and calcium deficiency puts you at risk of osteoporosis – a degenerative bone disorder not restricted to older women. When we feel the onset of flu, we buy anything with large amounts of vitamin C, and when we feel tired and lethargic, we pop vitamin B supplements.

New research has shown, too, that magnesium and calcium are absorbed better if bound to an ascorbate, citrate or amino acid chelate; vitamin C taken with meals improves iron absorption; vitamin D is needed for calcium absorption; and tannin in tea prevents assimilation of calcium, iron and zinc.

There are also many other products containing complex-sounding chemicals, amino acids, fatty-acids, antioxidants, proteins, enzymes and, more recently, joint-lubricating extracellular proteins.

Are all of these really necessary? Eating a balanced diet rich in a variety of fruits, vegetables, grains, dairy products and protein will meet most needs. But, as an athlete, your body's requirements for specific nutrients may not be met by diet alone. A multi-vitamin and multi-mineral supplement formulated for athletes is a good start – a guarantee that you are meeting the RDA. Taking additional calcium, magnesium and vitamin C supplements nightly before bed will relax hard-worked muscles and help you sleep. If you are vegetarian, diabetic or allergic to certain foods, consult a nutritionist to ensure your diet is balanced and your vitamin and mineral requirements are met.

Overconsumption of supplements can be dangerous. For example, excesses of the fat-soluble vitamins A, D, E and K are stored rather than eliminated, resulting in a greater potential for overdose and, while most mineral excesses are excreted in your urine, an excess of iron can lead to fatal poisoning.

Antioxidants

In response to stressors like air pollution, UV light, stress and exercise, the body produces an excess of free radicals, degrading healthy tissue. Reduced physical performance, ageing, compromised immune functioning, cancer and heart disease have been linked to free-radical damage. Fortunately, our bodies produce antioxidants to halt or inactivate free radicals and help repair cellular damage. As free radicals are partially responsible for muscle damage, soreness and reduced endurance, antioxidant supplementation is necessary. Antioxidants include vitamins and minerals absorbed from food (*see* below) and can also be taken as supplements.

Antioxidant	Where to find it	What it does
Vitamin C	citrus, guava, strawberry, kiwi, potato	promotes wound healing and iron absorption, and stimulates the immune system
Beta-carotene	carrots, apricots, leafy veg	helps to resist infection and neutralize free-radical damage
Vitamin E	vegetable oils, nuts, seeds	reverses some signs of ageing and other free-radical damage
Selenium	dairy, citrus, avocadoes	combats cellular damage, particularly of heart muscle
Copper	shellfish, liver, dried peas/beans, fruit, veg, nuts	helps body absorb and use iron
Zinc	meat, poultry, eggs, liver shellfish	stimulates the primary antioxidant enzyme manufactured by the body

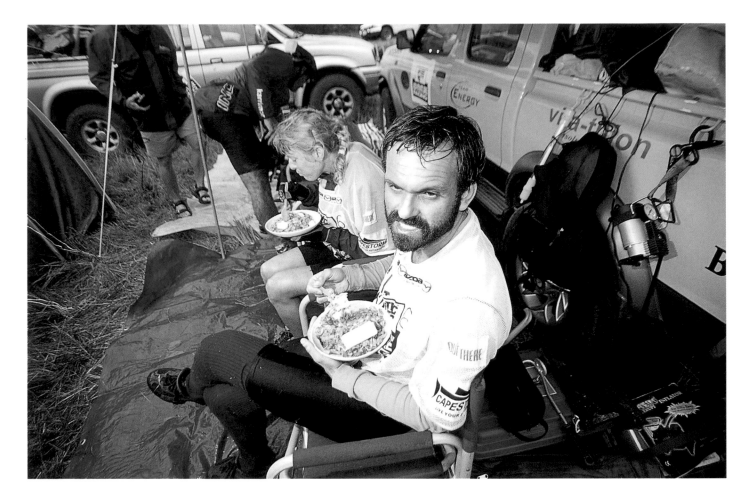

What should you eat?

Nutritionists wax lyrical about percentages, weights and calories without considering that: adventure racing is a multi-day, multi-discipline sport; we consider a six-hour event to be short; we are limited in the volume and weight of food we can carry; and that a scientifically formulated meal is useless unless we can get it down – and keep it down. So, while it is important to understand the benefits of proteins, carbohydrates and fats, a simple guideline is to eat a variety of foods you like. If they go down, your body will use them.

Here are some pointers:

- Your pre-event diet is important. A nutritionist can tailor a programme to suit your age, weight, lifestyle, activities and dietary preferences.
- During the race, eat a little every hour, and at least one substantial meal each day if possible.
- Consume a variety of foods.
- Consider the Glycaemic Index when planning your meals and snacks.
- Do not cut out fats.
- Remember to include protein, specifically vegetable proteins – such as nuts, legumes, lentils.
- Always carry enough food to last longer than you think you will be out in the field.
- Do not neglect nutrition on day one; you will never recover the deficit, affecting performance on day two and the remainder of the event.
- Carry some cash so you can buy fresh fruits, vegetables and tasty treats when available.
- Carry antacids and eat as needed while racing to avoid gastric distress.
- Post-event, give in to your cravings.
- Buy at least one sports publication to keep up with new research and nutritional trends.

TOP: **Easy-to-pack, high-energy foods make good choices for race meals. Here Team Energy takes a break to fuel up at one of the transition points during the Africa Adventure Quest 2001.**

Race food

Selecting food for a race can be challenging, and it gets increasingly difficult the longer the event. Over the last 20 years of racing I have found that the foods I like to eat vary constantly, but there are a few basics I can always rely on.

1. Try to choose food that looks like food. Energy bars and gels are excellent sources of nutrition, but you should not (and generally cannot) rely on them as your sole source of calories, especially in a long race.

2. Drink mostly water. Sports drinks can be useful to help maintain electrolyte balance in hot climates, but you should get the bulk of your fluids from straight water. The sugars in sports drinks cause dental problems and mouth ulcers after about a day, and you can get all the electrolytes you need from solid food.

3. Eat a balanced diet. Racing, especially over multiple days, is extremely taxing on your body and it can be difficult to eat meals that meet your nutritional requirements. Most athletes lose a lot of water through perspiration and other body functions during an event, in the process losing large quantities of water-soluble vitamins and minerals. To compensate, consider taking a multi-vitamin and/or multi-mineral supplement once a day.

4. Choose salty foods. The flavour most craved in long races is salt. This is often because many foods we choose are carbohydrate dense and we start to crave regular flavours. I like to eat potato chips, jerky and other savoury snacks as races get longer.

5. Ensure that you eat sufficient calories to keep pace with your energy expenditure. The longer the race and the lower your exercise intensity, the more fat and protein you will need to eat. For very short, fast races (that is to say, races of several hours or less), consume carbohydrates as your main energy source, with limited amounts of fat and protein, which can cause gastric distress.

Ian Adamson, Team Nike ACG / Balance Bar

ABOVE: With experience you will optimize your nutritional intake while choosing foods that are palatable. Packet soups, bread, muffins, dried meat, nuts and dried fruit are convenient options, with energy bars, sweets and chocolate for an energy kick.

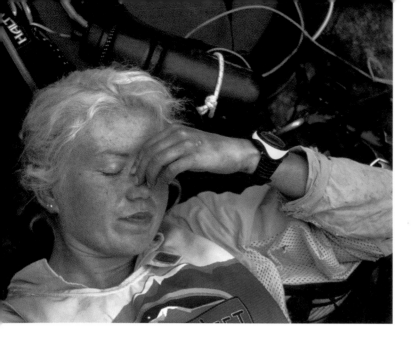

Medical know-how

Y OUR BODY CONSTITUTES a dynamic system that responds to external influences, striving to maintain a constant internal environment for the optimal functioning of cells, hormones and enzymes. The process of maintaining this constant state is referred to as homeostasis. When under excessive stress, the body reaches a point where it cannot respond and adapt to stressors – influences such as heat, cold, insufficient oxygen, food and water shortage, sleep deprivation, trauma and infection – that might affect the homeostatic balance. Subjected to similar stressors, some people show no sign of illness, strain or injury, while others may need medical intervention.

Although first-aid certification is not always required, everyone involved in AR should attend a first-aid class. A basic course teaches you life-saving skills such as assessing breathing and pulse, artificial respiration, cardiopulmonary resuscitation (CPR), stopping bleeding, immobilizing joints and bones, as well as patient support and maintenance while you wait for medical assistance. For a checklist of medical supplies to keep in your team's first-aid kit, see page 155.

Top first-aid tips:

1	Attend a first-aid course✓
2	Familiarize yourself with the symptoms, treatments and preventive methods for diseases endemic to the area you will be visiting✓
3	Carry all personal medications in the team's first-aid kit✓
4	Calm and reassure an injured person✓
5	Always send two people, not just one, to fetch medical assistance if required✓
6	Communication within the team is crucial. Deal with symptoms as soon as they start in order to avoid life-threatening situations✓

Medical assistance

Medical personnel are present at races to deal with medical emergencies. For all other complaints, your team should be self-supporting.

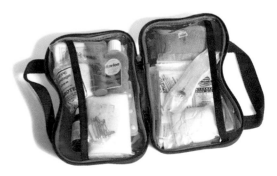

TOP: **Unless managed, physical and environmental stressors can jeopardize a team's race.**
INSET: **Use surgical gloves when attending to injuries in order to prevent infection.**
ABOVE RIGHT: **Every team is required to carry a first-aid kit during the race.**

Heat illnesses

Your body strives to sustain your body temperature at about 37°C (98.6°F). Three mechanisms ensure that metabolic and environmental heat are removed effectively: evaporative cooling; radiation (giving off heat); and convection (heat exchange from your body to the air). During exercise, food energy is utilized at a faster rate, generating more heat that must be removed. Evaporation accounts for most heat dissipation, affecting blood volume in the process, but cardiovascular responses are also essential. They are: increased cardiac output (heart rate and stroke volume) and temporary diversion of blood from the inner organs to the skin and muscles (vasodilation).

Sunburn (photodermatitis)

An inflammatory skin reaction due to overexposure to sunlight. Can be mild to severe depending on the duration of exposure and strength of solar UV radiation.

Symptoms: Skin feels hot to the touch, is often painful and appears red. Blistering may occur. Certain medications, including antibiotics and anti-inflammatories, may make the skin more photosensitive.

Treatment: Cool and soothe burning sensation with wet dressings. Apply after-sun lotion.

Prevention: Wear protective clothing (hat, long-sleeved shirts, long pants). Apply sunscreen regularly (SPF 25+).

Heat syncope

A brief fainting spell caused when blood pressure drops as a result of the vasodilation of blood vessels in response to a hot environment.

Symptoms: Weak feeling and blurred vision are common before the person falls down unconscious.

Treatment: Rest in a cool place; water and an electrolyte solution will ensure quick recovery.

Prevention: Ensure adequate hydration; avoid overexertion.

Heat cramps

Cramping and spasms in abdominal muscles and those most heavily used, i.e. hamstrings, quadriceps, gastrocnemius (calf), biceps and triceps.

Symptoms: Painful muscle cramps. Muscles feel hard and lumpy.

Treatment: Rest in a cool place; take water and an electrolyte solution.

Prevention: Ensure adequate hydration; avoid overexertion.

Heat exhaustion

Results from prolonged activity with inadequate electrolyte intake in a hot environment.

Symptoms: Fatigue, profuse sweating, headaches, dehydration and thirst, impaired judgement and inability to continue activity. Body temperature is raised slightly and heart rate at rest is elevated. Face is pale, cold and clammy.

Treatment: Rest, cooling and hydration. In severe cases intravenous fluids may be necessary. If sweating ceases, heat exhaustion may progress to heat stroke.

Prevention: Ensure adequate hydration; avoid overexertion.

Heat stroke

A life-threatening condition that results when the body's thermoregulatory mechanisms fail.

Symptoms: Rapidly rising body temperature, exceeding 40°C (104°F). Sweating ceases. Dizziness, weakness, confusion, blurred vision, convulsions, nausea, vomiting and weak pulse. Face is hot, flushed and dry. Unconsciousness results from hypotension (low blood pressure). In a race, the first sign may be irrational behaviour, sudden collapse and unconsciousness.

Treatment: Survival depends on rapid, whole-body cooling. Remove clothing and spray skin with water. Encourage evaporative cooling by fanning air across skin. Immersion in or sponging with cool water (not ice) is also effective. Once body temperature is reduced, lie the person on his/her side (recovery position) and monitor for changes. Get medical assistance.

Prevention: Ensure adequate hydration; avoid overexertion; and try to deal with minor symptoms before heat stroke develops.

ABOVE: From the discomfort of sunburn to the life-threatening condition of heat stroke, heat illnesses can be avoided by ensuring that you get adequate hydration, avoid overexertion and deal with minor symptoms before they escalate.

Cold illnesses

In response to cold, your body tries to conserve metabolic heat by reducing heat lost from the skin's blood vessels (vasoconstriction) and by generating metabolic heat through shivering. Immersion in water and exposure to cold and dry air can cause body temperature to drop to dangerously low levels. Avoid cold disorders by staying warm and dry. To keep warm, wear insulating layers of clothing and a windproof, waterproof shell, and keep your head covered. Layers provide more thermal insulation than one thick garment and can be added to or shed according to temperature and comfort. Avoid getting wet from either precipitation or sweat since wet clothing offers little insulation. Fabric should wick moisture away from the skin, keeping your body dry and allowing perspiration to evaporate. In cold conditions, dehydration is seldom considered, but should be. Skin blood vessel constriction results in a relative increase in central blood volume; the kidneys respond by removing more water from the blood, increasing urine volume, and speeding up dehydration.

Hypothermia

The most common cold disorder. Results from prolonged exposure or extreme cold, becoming increasingly severe in progressive stages.

Symptoms: Core body temperature below 35°C (95°F), greyish skin colour, slow and slurred speech, memory lapses, irritability, impaired co-ordination (unable to tie shoelaces or walk properly), drowsiness, exhaustion and inability to stand after sitting down. As severity increases, shivering ceases, breathing may stop and unconsciousness could result.

Treatment: Warm the person. Wrap him in a sleeping bag, climbing in to provide additional warmth. Give a warm drink if he is only mildly affected, is alert and can swallow.

If breathing stops, start artificial respiration, reducing the rate of ventilation to four to five breaths per minute. Get medical assistance.

Prevention: Keep warm and dry. Continued activity delays the onset of hypothermia but activity slows with growing fatigue and hypothermia will develop and worsen.

Frostnip, superficial frostbite and frostbite

Similar cold injuries of increasing severity. Freezing of the outer skin layer is followed by freezing of underlying tissues, even limbs. Fluid in and between cells crystallizes and ice crystals damage the cellular membranes, killing the cells.

Symptoms: Affected tissue appears white and is cold to the touch. There is inflammation and massive swelling (oedema) in more severe cases.

Treatment: Never rub or massage cold, injured tissues. Rewarming is effective; blow warm air on the skin or place the injured surface in close contact with a warm body area like an armpit. If someone with frostbite has to walk to get help, do not thaw the frozen limb. Additional damage will not occur provided the limb has not been thawed. Never thaw tissue by warming if it is likely to refreeze. Get medical assistance immediately.

Prevention: Keep all exposed skin covered. Keep warm and dry.

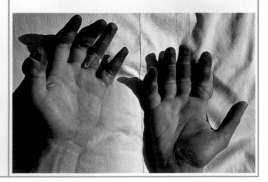

TOP: **A hot drink provides instant warmth when the symptoms of hypothermia are mild.**
ABOVE RIGHT: **The formation of ice crystals in and between cells (frostbite) is a serious conditions that can result in the loss of superficial tissue – even fingers, toes or limbs.**

Fluid imbalances

The amount of fluid lost through sweat depends on exercise intensity, humidity, environmental temperature and heat tolerance. Particularly in events where temperatures are high and activity continues for hours and days, the volume of fluid lost can exceed the average 0.8–1.4 litres/hr (28–50 fl oz/hr) – a volume greater than that excreted in urine. During exercise, the maximum amount of fluid that can empty from the stomach is 0.8–1.2 litres/hr (28–42fl oz/hr), so the balance between being sufficiently hydrated and dehydrated is obviously delicate.

hydration bladder

Dehydration

Caused by insufficient liquid intake.
Small fluid losses will not significantly decrease your performance, but losses greater than 2 per cent (about 1.5 litres or 53fl oz of sweat) will impair temperature regulation in a warm environment.

Symptoms: Hot, thirsty and fatigued. Dark-yellow urine. Low blood pressure. Heatstroke may develop.

Treatment: Water and rest. Intravenous fluids if severe.

Prevention: Drink even before you feel thirsty.

Hyponatraemia

Indicates low blood sodium levels, which can be caused by drinking too much, or by inadequate sodium intake and/or excessive sodium loss. Unlikely to be encountered in adventure races as water is not often readily accessible on the courses. This condition is potentially fatal.

Symptoms: Fatigue, bloating, nausea and disorientation.

Treatment: Water restriction and diuretics to encourage fluid and salt excretion.

Prevention: Drink according to thirst.

ABOVE: **With the exception of blisters, dehydration of varying severity is the most common medical condition treated by medics at adventure racing events. The administration of intravenous fluids is the best treatment for severe cases.**

Diarrhoeal disorders

As a healthy, active individual, it is unlikely that an increase in the frequency, fluidity and volume of your bowel movements is caused by anything other than a parasitic infection transmitted in contaminated food or water. Infection is common in areas with poor environmental sanitation. You may get diarrhoea with or without fever, blood and vomiting.

Symptoms: Diarrhoea, vomiting, headaches, dehydration, abdominal cramps.
- Traveller's diarrhoea (*Esterichia coli*): Incubation period 6–12hr. Onset is rapid and recovery is quick.
- Salmonella (*Salmonella enteritis*): Symptoms within 12hr. Recovery in 2–3 days.
- Cholera (*Vibrio cholerae*): Incubation period 1–5 days. Sudden onset. 'Rice water' stool. Severe water loss. Recovery within a week if infection is mild.
- Dysentry (*Shigella*): Incubation period 1–3 days. Sudden onset. Stool contains mucous and blood. Recovery in 3–7 days.

Treatment: Drink fluids to prevent dehydration. Note that anti-diarrhoeal drugs offer symptomatic relief but do not treat the infection and might prolong the illness. Antibiotics are not always effective, but may shorten the duration of symptoms.

Prevention: Boil it, cook it, peel it or leave it.

electrolyte powder for rehydration

Bone and joint injuries

Sprains and dislocations

A joint can be sprained or strained when the bones are moved beyond their normal range of movement and forced out of position. Supporting muscles, tendons and ligaments are stretched and/or torn.

Symptoms: Swelling, bruising, loss of movement. Dislocated joints appear deformed.

Treatment: 'Bind as you find', i.e. immobilize the joint. Get medical assistance.

Fractures

A break or crack in a bone. The surrounding skin may remain unbroken (closed fracture) or bone ends may protrude when fractures break the skin (open fracture).

Symptoms: Pain and tenderness, swelling and bruising. Arms and legs may be bent into an abnormal position. Discrepancy in limb length in femur (thigh) and humerus (upper arm) fractures.

Treatment: 'Bind as you find' – immobilize all fractures, unless the limb is bent at an abnormal angle, by securing the limb to a splint (trekking pole, stick). For open fractures, stop bleeding and dress wounds. Protect protruding bone without trying to reinsert it. Immobilize and get medical assistance.

TOP LEFT: **The greatest danger of diarrhoeal disorders is becoming dehydrated.**

TOP RIGHT: **Traversing uneven terrain demands constant concentration if you are to avoid injuries resulting from bad foot placement.**

Tissue damage

Bleeding

Mild or severe depending on the rate of bleeding and amount of blood lost. Severe blood loss initiates shock when inadequate oxygen is supplied to the brain and body tissues.

Symptoms: Pale, cold and clammy skin. Restlessness, apprehension, thirst, nausea, dizziness. Shallow breathing, rapid but weakening pulse. Unconsciousness may result if blood loss is great.

Treatment: Stop bleeding by applying pressure to the wound, elevating the bleeding part above heart level and allowing the person to rest in a sitting or lying position.

Infection

When injury exposes damaged tissue to the environment, infection may result from bacteria entering the wound.

Symptoms: Redness and inflammation around or streaking away from the wound. Skin feels firm, swollen and warm. As the infection advances, pus accumulates, causing yellow-green discoloration and discharge.

Treatment: In the field, a broad-spectrum antibiotic may clear up the infection; take the entire course of antibiotics as prescribed. If the infection does not clear but worsens, seek medical assistance.

Prevention: Clean wounds immediately. Sterile swabs are convenient and effective. Apply antiseptic ointments and clean dressings to protect from contamination. Tetanus vaccinations are advised every eight to 10 years.

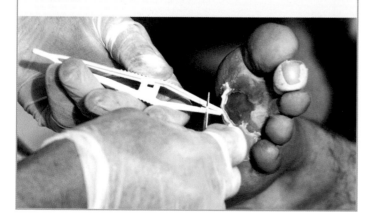

Fever

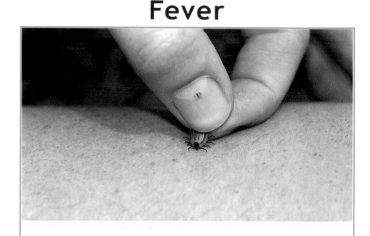

Fever is a fluctuation in body temperature – periodic attacks of chills, shivering and sweating, with elevated average body temperature (normal is about 37°C or 98.6°F). It occurs in response to parasitic and viral infections. A medical emergency arises when temperatures exceed 41°C (105.8°F).

Malaria is caused by the Plasmodium parasite, which is transmitted by an infected female Anopheles mosquito. Dengue and yellow fever are viral infections transmitted by the Aedes aegypti mosquito. Viral encephalitis (inflammatory disease of the brain) may be carried by ticks or mosquitoes. Tick-bite fever is common in Southern Africa. Incubation periods vary from 5–14 days.

Symptoms: Fever, headaches, dizziness, nausea, diarrhoea and vomiting.

Treatment: Supportive and symptomatic. Comfort patient and reduce temperature (see heat illnesses on page 123). Get medical help.

Prevention: Practise behavioural prevention: avoid insect bites by wearing protective clothing (long sleeves, leggings), applying insect repellent frequently and sleep (if you do sleep) under a bed-net impregnated with repellent. Always take anti-malaria drugs, which minimize the severity of infection and symptoms. Although there is no vaccine for many fevers, yellow fever vaccine protects effectively for at least 10 years.

TOP RIGHT: **Wear protective clothing to prevent bites from ticks, mosquitoes and other insects. Insect-borne parasites cause diseases such as malaria and tick-bite fever.**
ABOVE: **Wounds resulting from blisters are common and are open to infection.**

Bites and stings

Venomous stings

Stings by insects of the order Hymenoptera (wasps, hornets and bees) are common and are usually no cause for concern. But, in a sensitive person, one sting can cause an allergic reaction. Severity is variable.

Symptoms: Normal cases present with redness, itching and localized swelling. Symptoms of an allergic reaction include swelling around the eyes and mouth, nausea, vomiting, painful rash and difficulty in breathing.

Treatment: The stinger often remains and should be removed by teasing or scraping, not pulling. Apply an antihistamine ointment. Those with known sensitivity should carry an antihistamine kit. Get medical assistance.

Spider bites and scorpion stings

Symptoms: The toxin of most spider species causes local pain, redness and swelling. Black widow spider venom causes generalized muscular pains, muscle spasms and stiffness. Brown or violin spider bites cause little or no immediate pain. A lesion of dead tissue forms within 12 hours and continues to grow. Most scorpions are harmless, although some could cause localized pain. Centrurioides stings (in southwestern United States) cause immediate pain, muscle cramps, twitching, jerking, convulsions, increased respiration and weakness.

Treatment: Calm and reassure the person. Aim to relieve symptoms. Seek medical help.

false violin spider

Arthropod bites

Common biting and blood-sucking insects are ticks; sand-, horse-, blow- and tsetse-flies; fleas; lice; and mosquitoes. Many arthropods transmit disease-causing parasites, e.g. mosquito and malaria (see page 127). The larvae of some fly species burrow into the skin causing 'boils' or a telltale trail under the skin's surface.

Symptoms: Lesions vary from small, red, itchy bumps to large, painful ulcers.

Treatment: Remove ticks by applying a coat of Vaseline or paraffin. Apply some antihistamine cream to the lesions.

Prevention: Wear protective clothing and use insect repellents.

burrowing scorpion

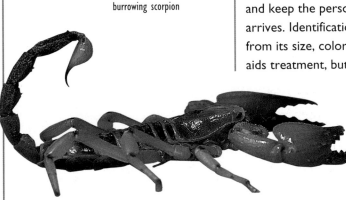

Snake bites

A venomous snake may spit or bite, though snakes may bite without injecting venom. Venom either attacks cells and tissues (cytotoxic) or interferes with the nervous system (neurotoxic).

Symptoms: Venom sprayed into the eyes causes immediate pain. Cytotoxic venom causes local and extensive tissue damage, swelling and internal bleeding. Neurotoxic venom causes breathing difficulties and paralysis. The person will go into shock.

Treatment: If eyes have been sprayed, flush with water immediately for 10min continuously. Anaesthetic eyedrops will soothe burning. For venomous bites, seek medical assistance immediately. Elevate the bite area above the heart. Calm, reassure and keep the person still until aid arrives. Identification of the snake from its size, coloration and markings aids treatment, but is not critical.

ABOVE: Bites and stings vary in severity, with even commonly occurring bee stings presenting problems for allergic individuals. The team's medical kit should include treatment for the full spectrum of bites and stings likely to occur in the race area.

Altitude

The higher you go, the less air there is above you to exert a force (air pressure) on your body. Thus, at high altitudes, air pressure is low and the air is 'thin', or less dense. Although there is the same amount of oxygen in the air at altitude and sea level, less is presented to your lungs at altitude. High-altitude sites are 1500–3500m (4920–11,480ft) above sea level and very-high-altitude locations are 3500–5500m (11,480–18,045ft) above sea level. Extreme altitude refers to any place above 5500m (18,045ft). Over time, the body can adapt to high-altitude conditions of 'thin air' and less oxygen by increasing respiration frequency, heart muscle mass and the rate of red blood cell production.

As illnesses result from incomplete acclimatization, risk is greater the faster you ascend and the longer you stay at altitude. Acute mountain sickness (AMS) results from rapid ascent. High-altitude pulmonary oedema and cerebral oedema are life-threatening altitude sicknesses.

Symptoms: Severe headache, fatigue, irritability, nausea, vomiting, constipation, decreased urine output with normal hydration, sleep disturbance.

Treatment: Immediate descent to lower altitudes, supplemental oxygen.

ABOVE: **Although the panoramic views at altitude are spectacular, be alert to the early signs of altitude sickness – headache, fatigue and nausea – in both yourself and the other members of your team.**

Foot care

Painful, blistered feet probably account for more race disappointments than any other illness or disorder. While there are no rules governing foot care, there are numerous ways to prevent foot problems. Jon Vonhof, author of *Fixing your Feet: Prevention and Treatment for Athletes*, and an authority on blisters, provides these useful tips.

Blisters

Blisters form when fluid accumulates between the inner and outer layers of your skin. They are encouraged by moisture, heat and friction. Hot spots – which are areas that become sore and red from rubbing – are precursors to blisters.

Treatment: Drain fluid-filled blisters, keeping the outer layer of skin, or 'roof', attached. Use a sterile needle or snip a 'V' in the side of the blister. Clean and dry before covering with plaster or duct tape. If the roof has ruptured, leave it on, laying it flat; apply antibiotic cream before patching.

Prevention:

- Ensure your shoes fit your feet; they may have to be a half-size or full-size larger than normal to accommodate swelling.
- Socks should wick moisture from your skin and must be changed frequently.
- Trim your toenails a week before the event.
- Air your feet at every opportunity to cool and dry the skin.
- Dirt is an irritant, so keep your feet clean. Gaiters prevent trail debris from entering shoes.
- Keep feet as dry as possible; moisture softens and macerates the skin, causing blisters.

- Toughen your skin by spending time on your feet in training, and using Tincture of Benzoin, methylated spirits and alcohol to dry and harden the skin.
- A dusting of powder keeps feet dry by absorbing moisture.
- Tape hot spots with a smooth plaster to reduce friction, avoid further rubbing and prevent blisters.

Moisture and cold management

Trench foot and immersion foot are often described together because in both conditions the foot becomes swollen, cold and numb. It also throbs and is incredibly painful as a result of blood vessel and nerve damage. Both conditions develop slowly over hours or even days, owing to the feet being exposed to moisture (either from water or perspiration). Whereas immersion foot is associated with cold water, trench foot occurs after walking for long periods with wet socks and shoes.

Treatment: Dry and warm feet. Elevate the feet above heart level to relieve swelling. Anti-inflammatory medication may help reduce swelling.

Prevention:

- Wear moisture-wicking socks (avoid 100 per cent cotton).
- Select shoes that drain quickly.
- Avoid socks and shoes that are too tight.
- Carry extra dry socks.
- Moisture-absorbing foot powders help keep your feet dry.
- When resting, remove socks and shoes to allow your feet to breathe and to dry out.
- Gently massage feet to promote circulation.

Lisa de Speville and Jon Vonhof

ABOVE: Good foot care and management techniques are acquired with experience. As you come into contact with different conditions and environments, you will learn how best to protect your feet and prevent blister formation.

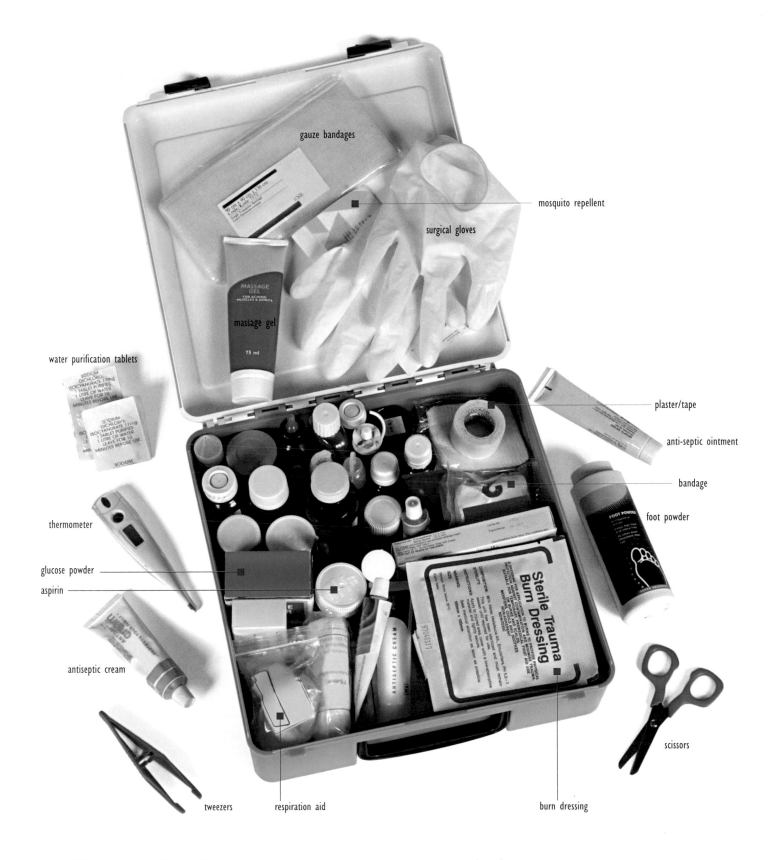

gauze bandages

mosquito repellent

surgical gloves

massage gel

75 ml

water purification tablets

plaster/tape

anti-septic ointment

bandage

foot powder

thermometer

glucose powder

aspirin

Sterile Trauma
Burn Dressing

antiseptic cream

scissors

tweezers   respiration aid   burn dressing

ABOVE: Although competitors will usually carry a basic first-aid kit, a more comprehensive medical kit should also be transported by the support crew. Transition points are the places to administer medical care before the next leg of the race begins.

Ten amazing races

ADVENTURE RACING DOES NOT fall within the bounds of a casual Saturday afternoon sporting spree. It transcends the bounds of mere challenge, moving into the realm of an adrenalin religion, drawing on the true grit of the human spirit and pitting competitors against back-to-back days of gruelling, expedition-style racing. It is a pursuit that pushes racers

beyond normally accepted levels of endurance, testing their physical, mental and emotional limits.

As in any dynamic and growing sport, this constant state of flux makes for an ever-changing and mouth-watering selection of choices on the global multi-

sport menu. Choosing 10 definitive events is a nigh impossible and, some might say, rather foolhardy task, as every racer is bound to have his or her own selection of must-do events. Ten races from around the globe have been chosen in the hope that this would give every reader a chance to enter at least one of the featured events. Read on and decide where in the world your next big race will be . . .

You will notice that two seminal events have not been included here. As far as the first of these, the Eco-Challenge, is concerned, comment regarding

Races highlighted in this chapter:

1. **Beast of the East:** Virginia

2. **Subaru Primal Quest:** USA

3. **Raid the North Extreme:** Canada

4. **Arctic Team Challenge:** Greenland

5. **High Coast 600:** Sweden

6. **Adrenalin Rush:** British Isles

7. **Expediçao Mata Atlantica:** Brazil

8. **Swazi Xtreme:** Swaziland, Southern Africa

9. **Southern Traverse:** South Island, New Zealand

10. **Mild Seven Outdoor Quest:** Sabah, Borneo

future developments has been rather vague and the best way to stay updated would be to check their website regularly at www.ecochallenge.com. Raid Gauloises headquarters has been more forthcoming

TOP: **Television crews and photojournalists follow competing teams during a camel-trekking leg of the Global Extreme event held in the Kalahari Desert in Southern Africa.**
INSET: **Extreme fatigue is just one obstacle racers must deal with during an expedition race.**

and a recent media release gave a clear indication of where this event is headed. Certainly one of adventure racing's seminal events, the Raid has experienced a rapid transformation during the more than two decades since its inception, morphing from its original format to incorporate the X-Adventure Raid Series.

However, the constant evolution of AR sees organizers ringing the changes again as from 2004 with the creation of the Raid World Championships. Despite the new format, organizers Saga d'Aventures will strive to maintain the original spirit that has established the Raid Gauloises as one of the world's premier adventure races, continuing to present challenging events in the most remote corners of the planet. The year 2003 was ear-marked as one 'of transition' for a race many athletes refer to only as The Raid and, although the X-Adventure events in France/Italy, the United States, Spain and New Caledonia went ahead, the Raid Gauloises scheduled for Peru was cancelled and race rules were revised to accommodate these changes.

ABOVE: The Austrians of Briko Adventure Team Tirol tackle the paddling section of the Raid Gauloises 2002 in northern Vietnam using a traditional bamboo raft over 7m (23ft) long. The event was the longest in the Raid Gauloises' history at 1008km (630 miles).

1. Beast of the East

Where: **Eastern USA**

Entry fee: **US$2800 per four-person team**

Distance: **560km (350 miles)**

Fastest time: **80hrs (Team Eco Internet)**

Disciplines: **Canoeing (lake and whitewater), trekking, trail running, fixed-rope courses, mountain biking, whitewater swimming, mountaineering river crossings and orienteering**

Race & terrain description: **Competitors will experience everything from explosive whitewater along scenic rivers to magnificent fixed-rope courses throughout the eastern USA. Expect superb trekking and mountain biking along historic Civil War roads. The topography is steep and rugged, covering some of the highest peaks in eastern USA. Anyone taking on the Beast of the East can count on a demanding but beautiful race.**

Biggest wow factor: **One of North America's original adventure races**

Organizers: **Don Mann, Odyssey Adventure Racing**

Contact: **tel +91-757-6453397; info@oarevents.com www.oarevents.com**

ABOVE: River crossings during Odyssey Adventure Racing's Beast of the East 2000, which was held in the challenging West Virginian landscape, necessitated protective headgear and the use of flotation options.

2. Subaru Primal Quest

Where:	**Various locations in USA**
Entry fee:	**US$6500**
Distance:	**720km (450 miles)**
Fastest time:	**Five days**
Disciplines:	**Caving, mountain biking, flat-water paddling, whitewater paddling, hiking, orienteering, ropes (including rappelling, ascending, Tyrolean traverse)**
Race & terrain description:	**The ultimate in non-stop multi-sport team competition, using teamwork, conditioning and the ability to adapt to change in an effort to complete the secret course.**
Biggest wow factor:	**Many crown jewels of the Sierra Nevada mountains yield an amazing ropes section, and some of the best paddling in the USA.**
Organizers:	**Dan Barger, Primal Quest**
Contact:	**tel +91-408-9973581; dan@ecoprimalquest.com**

ABOVE: Sometimes, even during hardcore races such as the 2003 Subaru Primal Quest, you will find yourself cranking along tarmac roads. Investigate the option of smooth tyres to improve your cycling speed in situations such as these.

3. Raid the North Extreme

Where: Various locations in Canada

Entry fee: US$2800

Distance: 500km+ (310 miles)

Fastest time: 88hr 21min (Team Salomon-Eco-Internet)

Disciplines: Trekking, mountain biking, sea and lake kayaking, dory rowing, rope work and navigation

Race & terrain description: At least five to six days of non-stop racing. The route traverses various locations in Canada, at times stabbing into its rugged wilderness interior. Outstanding along the way are the extremely challenging lake and sea kayak legs, very technical navigation, long stretches of remote, wild country and enough decision-making to keep competitors constantly on their toes.

Biggest wow factor: Sea kayaking among icebergs and whales

Organizers: Geoff Langford, Frontier Adventure Racing

Contact: info@far.on.ca; geoff@far.on.ca

ABOVE: Frontier Adventure Racing is well known for pulling out all the stops in presenting exciting and challenging events. Testimony to this is the zip-wire crossing at Atikokan during the 2003 Raid the North Extreme in Ontario, Canada.

4. Arctic Team Challenge

Ammassalik Island (Greenland)

Where: Ammassalik Island, East Greenland

Entry fee: 42,000DK (inclusive of some flights, travel and accommodation)

Distance: 260km (160 miles)

Fastest time: 30hr 16min
(Team Peak Performance)

Disciplines: Ice fjord paddling, glacier- and off-track trekking, climbing, mountain biking. Partly stage and expedition race, the ATC is always presented in late July – the height of the Arctic summer

Race & terrain description: The route is set in one of the most isolated human settlements on earth. To the west lies the icecap and to the east the solid fields of ice of the Polar Sea, which obstruct navigation for about seven months of the year. This is a spectacular and dramatic event set in one of the planet's most challenging landscapes.

Biggest wow factor: Paddling among 1000-year-old icebergs on Sermilik fjord

Organizers: Anders Stenbakken and Hans Christian Florian, Arctic Team Challenge

Contact: tel +9299-299-981311;
atc@greennet.gl; www.atc.gl

ABOVE: **Team 66° North from Iceland traverses the extreme mountain terrain of east Greenland during the Arctic Team Challenge 2003. Race regulations allowed teams to leave their packs at an earlier checkpoint to alleviate safety concerns during an ascent of the region's highest peak.**

5. High Coast 600

Where: Hoga Kusten region, Sweden

Entry fee: 15,000 Swedish Krone per team

Distance: 600km (373 miles)

Fastest time: 94hr 6min (Team Arkitektkopia)

Disciplines: Trekking, mountain biking, fixed ropes (including via ferrata), sea kayaking, coast-eering, swimming, canoeing, in-line skating, navigation

Race & terrain description: Takes place along Sweden's High Coast region, with teams of four racing a challenging route traversing a scenic area of dense forests, towering peaks, tranquil lakes and an unspoilt archipelago. Although it is a long race, well-placed transitions and variable leg distances make it a speedy, hard-fought duel between top teams from all over Northern Europe.

Biggest wow factor: Panoramic kayaking along the High Coast archipelago

Organizers: Mikael Nordström and Helena Lind, High Coast 600

Contact: tel +946-660-73110; helenalind2000@hotmail.com

ABOVE: During the final stage of the High Coast 600, two paddlers from Team Arkitektkopia approach the bridge from which the other two members of their team are required to make an 80m (260ft) abseil into the kayaks before they can paddle to the finish line.

6. Adrenalin Rush

Where: British Isles

Entry fee: US$2200 (GBP1600)

Distance: 420–485km (260–300 miles)

Fastest time: 75hr 50m (Team The North Face, 2003)

Disciplines: Trekking, fixed ropes, horse riding, kayaking, climbing, mountain biking, swimming, canyoning, navigation and usually a secret discipline, e.g. archery, liloteering, or caber tossing

Race & terrain description: This is Europe's toughest expedition-style adventure race. The format is non-stop and unsupported. The route of the seven-day event is across the British Isles' most imposing mountain ranges. Water stages are uncompromising, with kayakers taking to rivers, lochs and the seas. Spectacular climbing sections include jumaring, abseiling and often a Tyrolean traverse. Each year the race is located in a different part of the United Kingdom or Ireland.

Biggest wow factor: Whitewater lilo glide down the Falls of Leny

Organizers: Brian Elliot, Adventure Sports One

Contact: tel +44-28406-22044; brian.elliott@tibus.com www.adrenalinrush.co.uk

ABOVE: **Team Reebok Adventure tackles a tough trekking section of the Adrenalin Rush in Ireland. From left: Mikael Nordström, Swedish High Coast 600 organizer; Christoffer Åshammar; and expedition traveller Magnus Persson, holder of the world record for the fastest unsupported ski crossing of Greenland.**

7. Expediçao Mata Atlantica

Where: **Brazil, South America**

Entry fee: **±US$1500**

Distance: **±500km (310 miles)**

Fastest time: **116hr 40min (Team Epinephrine)**

Disciplines: **Navigation, trekking, fixed ropes, swimming, mountain biking, paddling (Canadian and dugout canoes and/or inflatable kayaks)**

Race & terrain description: **Competitors traverse liana jungles where sunlight never penetrates, *cerrado* (open pasture with stunted vegetation), rocky elevations and overgrown forest streams with trees hundreds of years old. Rafting stages follow previously unexplored rivers through rapids and large waterfalls. Although the mountain-biking stages are not too technical, they are long, following dirt roads through cattle-ranch country.**

Biggest wow factor: **Navigating the primeval Amazon jungle in the dark**

Organizers: **Alexandre Freitas, Sociedade Brasileira de Corridas de Aventura**

Contact: **ema@ema.com.br**
www.corridadeaventura.com.br

ABOVE: **Energetic competitors dash off at the start of the 2001 Expediçao Mata Atlantica in the Amazon jungle in Brazil. The EMA allows racers from around the world to test their mettle within the gruelling Amazon environment.**

8. Swazi Xtreme

Swaziland

Where:	**Kingdom of Swaziland**
Entry fee:	**ZAR2500 per four-member mixed team**
Distance:	**200–250km (125–155-mile) Pro Event and 80–120km (50–75-mile) Sport Event**
Fastest time:	**35hr 15min (Team Tsunami)**
Disciplines:	**Hiking/running, mountain biking, white-water rafting/canoeing/tubing, fixed ropes, canyoning, swimming, caving and navigation**
Race & terrain description:	**The Swazi Xtreme regularly passes through national parks, and teams will be briefed on procedures required when encountering elephant, rhino, buffalo, hippo, crocodile, leopard and even lion. Diverse terrain features more streams and rivers per square kilometre than any other country in Africa. Midnight abseils off towering peaks, tube rides along plunging gorges, off-trail trekking through montane woodland and crawling along ancient caverns will make this a race to remember.**
Biggest wow factor:	**Extreme landscapes and the friendly support of the local people**
Organizers:	**Darron Raw, Swazi Trails/Raw Africa**
Contact:	**darron@rawafrica.com**

ABOVE: **Team Linden Cycles tackles the granite Etjedze Rock in the Mkhondvo River Valley in 2003. Once its deeply criss-crossing interior chimneys had been climbed, a 40m (130ft) abseil was the only way down.**

9. Southern Traverse

South Island
(New Zealand)

Where: The South Island, New Zealand

Entry fee: NZ$6000

Distance: 400–500km (250–310 miles)

Fastest time: 96hr 33min (Propeller Heads)

Disciplines: Varies, but will probably include mountain-, snow- and glacier trekking, mountain biking, kayaking, rafting, coasteering and orienteering

Race & terrain description: This technical course designed by top international racer Geoff Hunt is a perennial favourite with multi-sport endurance athletes. Expect navigation and terrain to be harsh, following demanding off-trail treks, mountain-biking legs along trails, and kayak sections on both natural lakes and whitewater rivers. No wonder it has gained a reputation as New Zealand's (and arguably the world's) most formidable expedition race.

Biggest wow factor: The opportunity to race the top Kiwis on their home turf

Organizers: Geoff Hunt and Pascale Lore, Southern Traverse

Contact: tel +64-3-4418215; info@southerntraverse.com

ABOVE: Tired competitors use trekking poles to negotiate the extreme slopes of the spectacular Marlborough Sounds during the Southern Traverse 2002. Team Seagate from New Zealand, captained by Nathan Fa'ave, won the event in a time of 97 hours and 13 minutes.

10. Mild Seven Outdoor Quest

Sabah, Borneo (Malaysia)

Where: **Sabah, Malaysian Borneo**

Entry fee: **US$8000 per team**

Distance: **300km (185 miles)**

Fastest time: **25hr (estimated winning time)**

Disciplines: **Seven sporting disciplines: mountain biking, kayaking, in-line skating, adventure skills, paddling, running, team biathlon**

Race & terrain description: **This four-day stage race challenges the endurance and strength of the world's best athletes while offering spectacular views of nature at its finest. Various race legs are planned for each day, allowing racers to pit their minds and bodies against each other and their environment.**

Biggest wow factor: **Cultural interaction with local population**

Organizers: **Promotional Campaigns (Asia) and IMG**

Contact: **Race organizer: IMG tel +852-2131-0228; teresa.hong@ogilvy.com**

ABOVE: Danelle Ballangee of Team Hi-Tec (right) stares down her perennial rival Elina Mäki-Rautila of Team Nokia at the start of the second day of the Mild Seven Outdoor Quest in Kota Kinabalu, Borneo. The Hi-Tec team went on to win the event, successfully defending their title.

Check lists   pp = per person   pt = per team

CORE SHORT-COURSE KIT ITEMS

SWIMMING/WATER LEG

Swimming goggles ☐
Swimming trunks ☐
Earplugs ☐
Fins ☐
Wetsuit ☐

TRAIL RUNNING

All-terrain trail runners ☐
Extra laces ☐
Running socks ☐
Quick-dry, non-chafe shorts ☐
Breathable wicking top ☐
Outer shell jacket ☐

MOUNTAIN BIKING

Hard-tail bicycle with front suspension and clip-in pedals ☐
Bike computer ☐
Cycling helmet ☐
Bike tools (pump, tyre levers, chain breaker, spare tube, multi-tool) ☐
SPD cycling shoes ☐
Cycling clothes (top, socks and padded pants) ☐
Gloves ☐
Light ☐
Tow system ☐

OTHER

Backpack with hydration system ☐
Cap with neck protection ☐
Eyewear ☐
Suntan lotion ☐
Energy bars and/or trail snacks ☐

CORE KIT FOR LONGER RACES

MOUNTAIN BIKING

1. Compulsory (pp)
Helmet ☐
Mountain bike ☐
2. Recommended (pt)
Bike lights ☐
Repair kit: spare tubes, tyre levers, puncture repair kit, multi-tool, chain breaker tool, pump, valve spanner
Cable ties ☐
Odometers ☐
Watches ☐

PADDLING

1. Compulsory (pp)
PFD ☐
Paddles ☐
Whistle ☐
2. Recommended (pp)
Dry-bags ☐
Windproof splash-proof outer shell ☐
Wetsuit booties/shoes ☐
Paddle leash ☐
Helmet ☐
In wet/cold weather:
3mm wetsuit ☐
Thermal shirt and long pants ☐
Beanie or balaclava ☐
Non-slip gloves ☐
3. Compulsory (pt)
Throw rope (min. 10m/33ft); 1–2 ☐
Flares ☐
4. Recommended (pt)
A paddle-specific hydration bladder ☐
Cable ties ☐
Duct tape ☐

HIKING

1. Compulsory (pp)
Whistle ☐
Torch/headlamp ☐
Windproof outer shell ☐
Food for 24 hours ☐
Minimum 4l (7pt) water capacity ☐
2. Recommended (pp)
Gloves for rope work, hiking in thick bush ☐
Gaiters ☐
Spare batteries ☐
Hiking poles ☐
Protective hat for sun ☐
Beanie/balaclava for cold ☐
3. Compulsory (pt)
Sleeping bag (1–2) ☐
Bivvy bag (preferably 2) ☐
2 emergency/space blankets ☐
Lock-blade knife ☐
Shelter ☐
10m (33ft) safety rope ☐
Compass ☐
Light/smoke flares ☐
First-aid kit (see separate section) ☐
4. Recommended (pt)
Lighter ☐
Cable ties ☐
Local currency ☐
Wet/cold weather
Waterproof raincoat ☐
Waterproof rain pants ☐
Thermal shirt ☐
Waterproof gloves ☐
Warm pants/tights ☐
Waterproof socks ☐

MOUNTAINEERING (pp)

Climbing harness ☐
2 screw-gate carabiners ☐
Helmet ☐
Descending device ☐
2 prussiks ☐
2 slings ☐

NAVIGATION

Full set of maps ☐
Protractor ☐
Pencil ☐
Waterproof colour pens ☐
Highlighters ☐
Small ruler ☐
Long ruler ☐
Scissors ☐
Eraser ☐
Calculator ☐
Map distance measurer ☐
Compass ☐
Altimeter ☐
Map bag ☐
Bike map carrier ☐
GPS (if allowed) ☐

SUPPORT CREW

VEHICLE EQUIPMENT

2x4 or 4x4 truck/van ☐
Spare tyre ☐
Jack (may need high-lift) ☐
Compressed air in can ☐
Spanners ☐
Towrope ☐
Jumper cables ☐
Reflective triangle ☐
Jerrycan of fuel ☐
Spare trailer tyre ☐
Roof rack, bike rack and boat rack ☐

BICYCLE SPARES (pt)

6 inner tubes ☐
4 skewers ☐
Tyre liners ☐
Puncture repair kits ☐

2 brake pads ☐
Spoke spanner ☐
Allen-key set ☐
2 brake cables ☐
2 gear cables ☐
4 spare spokes ☐
2 chains ☐
Chain-breaker ☐
Chain lubricant ☐
Cloth for cleaning ☐

CAMPING GEAR
Waterproof shelter ☐
(pop-up gazebo with
side panels or tent big
enough to stand in)
3 tarpaulins ☐
Mattresses (if space) ☐
4 sleeping bags ☐
Pillows ☐
2 small fold-up tables ☐
4 fold-up chairs ☐
Plastic packing crates ☐
with lids (1–2 per racer)
2-plate gas cooker ☐
Spare gas ☐
2 cooler boxes (1 for ☐
everyday items, 1 for
frozen goods)
Camping fridge (luxury) ☐
Gas lamp with spare ☐
mantles and/or
rechargeable battery-
operated lights
Headlamps ☐
Water containers: ☐
75l (20gal)
2 thermos flasks ☐
1 x 10m (33ft) rope ☐
and tie-downs

COOKING EQUIPMENT
Kettle ☐
2 large pots ☐

Frying pan ☐
Wooden spoon ☐
Bread knife ☐
Sharp knife ☐
Breadboard ☐
Can opener ☐
Serving spoon ☐
4 cutlery sets ☐
4 bowls ☐
4 tin/plastic ☐
mugs/cups/glasses
Tin/plastic/paper ☐
plates
Barbecue grid ☐

DISHES AND LAUNDRY
Washing tub ☐
Washing cloth/sponge ☐
Drying cloth ☐
Dishwashing liquid ☐
Laundry detergent ☐
Rope and clothes pegs ☐

FOOD CHECK LIST
Drinks
Milk ☐
Coffee ☐
Tea ☐
Hot chocolate, etc. ☐
Fruit juice ☐
Drinking water ☐
Carbonated beverages ☐
Fruit
Bananas ☐
Oranges ☐
Tangerines ☐
Apples ☐
Watermelon ☐
Sweet melon ☐
Grapes ☐
Meat (pre-/semi-
cooked /smoked
products last longer)
Salami ☐

Smoked bacon and/or ☐
bacon bits
Gammon ☐
Boiled ham ☐
Canned tuna ☐
Other preserved meats ☐
Other
Cereals and/or ☐
porridge
Yoghurt ☐
Eggs ☐
Pasta ☐
Pasta sauces ☐
Soup (tinned/packet) ☐
Bread and/or rolls ☐
Cheese ☐
Tomatoes ☐
Small potatoes ☐
Rice ☐
Dried fruit ☐
Nuts ☐
Sandwich ☐
fillings/spreads
Powdered milk ☐
and/or preserved
sweetened milk
Sugar ☐
Salt and pepper ☐
Ziploc™ bags ☐

**ALL-PURPOSE
ESSENTIALS**
Extra compass ☐
Duct tape ☐
Cable ties ☐
Permanent marker ☐
Toilet paper ☐
Matches and lighter ☐
Firelighters ☐
Spade ☐
Garbage bags ☐
Plastic bags of all sizes ☐
Binoculars ☐

**MEDICAL/
FIRST-AID KIT**
Anti-inflammatory gel, ☐
tablets and patches
Anti-bacterial cream ☐
Anti-histamine cream ☐
Anti-histamine tablets ☐
Headache tablets ☐
Band-aids ☐
Broad-spectrum ☐
antibiotic for infected
wounds
Stretch-fabric plasters ☐
Duct tape ☐
Second skin ☐
Strapping tape ☐
Cotton wool ☐
Gauze ☐
Triangle bandage ☐
Massage oil (Arnica) ☐
Disinfectant solution ☐
Sterile/alcohol swabs ☐
Friars Balsam ☐
Eyedrops ☐
Scissors ☐
Tweezers ☐
2 knee guards ☐
2 ankle guards ☐
Rehydration (elec- ☐
trolyte) sachet
Earbuds/Q-Tips ☐
Insect repellent ☐
Sunscreen (SPF 25+) ☐
After-sun lotion ☐
Aqueous cream ☐
Vaseline ☐
Surgical gloves ☐
Small syringe ☐
and needles (for
draining blisters)
Heat packs ☐
Ice packs ☐
Water purifier ☐

Glossary

Abseiling: using fixed rope and friction devices for controlled descent of a steep cliff (see also 'rappelling')

Belay: safety rope attached to a climber to arrest an accidental fall

Bivvy bag: waterproof body bag for protection against wind and rain. Used instead of a tent

Canyoneering: negotiating a gorge, ravine or canyon by scrambling, swimming, wading, rock-hopping, etc; also called canyoning, kloofing

Carabiner: metal snap-ring device with a spring-loaded gate that opens to attach to ropes, equipment, harnesses, etc.

Chine: V-shaped angle of the boat where the bottom and side intersect

Classic (event): adventure race over two days, covering ±250km (155 miles), and incorporating multiple disciplines and navigation

Coasteering: navigating the shoreline of the ocean or a major inland body of water

Contour lines: topographical lines on a map joining points of equal altitude above mean sea level

Control points/checkpoints: physical locations that must be visited by all participants during a race

Co-ordinates: longitude and latitude information on a map to indicate your position North or South of the equator and East or West of the international dateline

Dark zone: period, usually from sunset to sunrise, when competitors must stop – for safety reasons

Dry-bag: waterproof polythene storage bag

Eskimo roll: body manoeuvre allowing a paddler to right a capsized kayak without disembarking

Expedition race: multi-day race of more than 400km (250 miles); competitors may be assisted by a support crew, or compete unassisted

Figure 8: friction device shaped like a figure 8 used in mountaineering

Flying fox: see Tyrolean traverse

Glissade: descending a snow slope in a controlled slide

Hard-pack: well-compacted dirt- or gravel-road surface

Hard-tail: mountain bike with front suspension forks, but no rear suspension

Hitting the wall/bonking: running out of energy during a race, sometimes to the extent of being unable to continue

Hole: formed when fast-moving water flows over a drop and circulates back upon itself to cause a possible water trap; also called a hydraulic

Hot spot: red, sensitive area caused by friction between the skin of your feet and debris in your shoes or a sock fold; precursor of a blister

Hydration: fluid needed to maintain physical activity and prevent dehydration through excessive sweating during long events in high temperatures

Hypoglycaemia: low blood sugar level

Hyponatraemia: low blood sodium levels

Hypothermia: when core body temperature drops below 35°C/95°F

Jumaring: ascending a free-hanging rope using a toothed metal clamp and slings

Layering: wearing garments in various layers

Magnetic North: the North to which your compass needle points

Multi-tool: pocket-sized utility tool with knife blades, screwdrivers, bottle openers, etc.

Passport: laminated, waterproof card that must be clipped or marked at passport control points (checkpoints) to confirm completion of the full course

PFD: personal flotation device worn by paddlers

Portage: carrying a boat/bike

Rappelling: see abseiling

Rocker: curve at the bow and stern of a kayak; a less pronounced curve means more speed, better tracking, but less manoeuvrability

Self-arrest: self-rescue manoeuvre using an ice axe to arrest a slide down a snow or ice slope

Singletrack: narrow section of trail (usually in mountain biking) where you can only ride in single file

Soft-tail: dual-suspension mountain bike with front and rear shocks

SPD shoes: Shimano Pedalling Dynamics – a clip-in mountainbike shoe that attaches the shoe to the pedal

Spray-deck: polythene or neoprene waterproof skirt fitted to the body and over the kayak cockpit as protection from the elements

Sprint (event): short (1–4hr) multi-disciplinary, off-road race incorporating mountain biking, swimming/paddling and running

Stage races: racers compete over specified distances each day, sleeping overnight

Transition: physical point where race disciplines change, e.g. between mountain biking and paddling

True North: 'top' of the earth, the North Pole, where the lines of longitude meet

Tyrolean traverse: fixed rope traverse between two points across a river or gorge while attached by harnesses and friction devices; may require you to haul yourself up by muscle power; also known as a flying fox or zip-wire

Urban challenge: AR event staged within a metropolitan area, using the city landscape

Via ferrata: in situ fixed-rope course along ledges/cliffs, across ravines and through whitewater

Waypoints: features like streams, bridges and mountain peaks en route to a target, which confirm your location; also called attack points

Wick: moves moisture away from the skin, dispersing it from the surface of a garment through evaporation

Wipe-out: big fall

Recommended websites and further reading

www.4windsadventure.com All about Four Winds Adventure, which presents the USA Supreme Adventure Race

www.adventuresportsmagazine.com Adventure Sports Magazine is arguably the world's foremost multi-sport publication

www.adventureteam.com Adventure Team Outdoor Sports Clubs is a diverse, multi-sport web resource

www.ar.co.za The definitive website on AR in Africa

www.arfe.org Adventure Racers for the Environment pulls together aspects of interest to adventure racers with an environmental conscience

www.argear.com Seeking AR gear? You will find it here...

www.arauki.co.za The AR Association of UK and Ireland website highlights events and concerns in these countries and has useful links to British, European and global sites and races

www.asportsone.com Site of the UK's top AR event, the Adrenalin Rush, organized by Adventure Sports One

www.atc.gl Find out more about the unique East Greenland terrain in which the Arctic Team Challenge takes place

www.axn-asia.com A portal with links to Asian adventure racing and outdoor sporting events

www.checkpointzero.com Great A news, calendar, store and chat group site

www.ecochallenge.com The official Eco-Challenge site, unarguably the AR event with the biggest worldwide following

www.ecoprimalquest.com All you ever wanted to know about the prestigious Subaru Primal Quest, currently the AR event with the highest prize money in the world

www.highcoast600.com Scandinavia's premier adventure race, presented in the scenic Hoga Kusten region of Sweden

www.lnt.org The Leave No Trace website promotes responsible outdoor recreation

www.msoq.com The Mild Sevens Outdoor Quest is one of Asia's most talked-about adventre racing events

www.oarevents.com Website of the organizer of the awesome Beast of the East and a range of other adventure events

www.racingahead.com Homepage of the organizer of the Appalachian Extreme and a range of other events

www.raidgauloises.com All about the granddaddy of AR, now presented in a new format

www.raidthenorth.com The site of Frontier Adventure Racing, organizer of Raid the North and the Salomon Adventure Challenge

www.railriders.com Much more than a gear and clothing site, Railriders offers links to many AR resources

www.sleepmonsters.com Internationally renowned international AR web resource with links to major events

www.southerntraverse.com All you want to know about New Zealand's world-famous flagship AR event

www.usara.com Official site of the United States Adventure Racing Association

www.worldar.com Full AR resource site covering everything from tips and techniques to finding a teammate

www.worldclassteams.com Get into the AR mode with top AR racer Robyn Benincasa's team-building organization

Addison, G. (2000). *Whitewater Rafting: The Essential Guide to Equipment and Techniques*. London: New Holland Publishing.

Armstrong, L.E. (1999). *Performing in Extreme Environments*. Illinois: Human Kinetics.

Bell, D.R. (2000). *Tropical Medicine*. London: Blackwell Science.

Burke, E.R. and Gastelu, D. (1999). *Avery's Sports Nutrition Almanac*. New York: Avery Publishing Group.

Caldwell, L. and Siff, B. (2001). *Adventure Racing – The Ultimate Guide*. Colorado: Velo Press.

Girard Eberle, S. (2000). *Endurance Sport Nutrition*. Illinois: Human Kinetics.

Hattingh, G. (1998). *The Climber's Handbook*. London: New Holland Publishing.

Hattingh, G. (2001). *The Outdoor Survival Manual*. London: New Holland Publishing.

Letham, L. (1996). *GPS Made Easy: Using Global Positioning Systems in the Outdoors*. Winnipeg: Rocky Mountain Books.

Loots, J. (2000). *Sea Kayaking: The Essential Guide to Equipment and Techniques*. London: New Holland Publishing.

Mann, D. and Schaad, K. (2001). *The Complete Guide to Adventure Racing*. New York: Hatherleigh Press.

Tierney, L.M., McPhee, S.J. and Papadakis, M.A. (1994). *Current Medical Diagnosis and Treatment*. New Jersey: Prentice Hall.

Index

abseiling (rappelling) 66, **76**
  safety 67
Acute Mountain Sickness (AMS)
  129
Adamson, Ian **12**, **14**, 15, **29**
Adrenalin Rush 144–145
Adventure Quest Africa 25
Alaska Wilderness Mountain
  Challenge 9
Allen keys **36**
altitude 129
aluminium open canoes **56**
amino acids 114
Amundsen, Roald 8
antioxidants 119
AR shoes **40**
AR shoes, mountain-bike **40**
Arctic Team Challenge 140–141
arthropod bites 128
backpack, choosing a **42–44**
  features **43**
balaclava **74**
Ballangee, Danelle **153**
basic gear and equipment 39
bearing 100–101
Beast of the East 10, **134–135**
belays, direct **66**
  indirect **66**
Benincasa, Robyn **12**, **87**
beta-carotene 119
bicycle pump **54**
bites and stings 128
bleeding 127
blisters **41**, 130
bone joint injuries 126
'bonking' 116 see also 'hitting the
  wall'
Briko Adventure Team Tirol **133**
bungy cord **54**
Burnett, Mark 10, **11**, **12**, 14
burrowing scorpion **128**
calories 121
canyoning 76
canyons 89
carabiner **68**
carbohydrate bars 118
carbohydrate-electrolyte drinks
  116, **117**, 118

carbohydrates 28, 115
climbing helmet **68**
clothing 36, 37
  deserts 38
  rainforests and wetlands 38
  sub-zero environments 38
coasteering 77
cold illnesses 124
compass 36, **100**
copper 119
Course des Trois Sports 9 see
  also Race of Three Sports
craft, traditional 81
crampons **74**
cross-country skiing 70
crossing training 46
cycling computer 20
  helmet **80**
  shorts 54
dehydration 125
Desert Challenge (2001) 77
Desert Challenge (Namib) 48
desert gear and equipment 50
  cap **50**
  Railrider **50**
  survival blanket **50**
  water purification tablets **50**
desert trekking tips 50
  navigation 50
  shoes and socks 50
  temperature 50
  trekking poles **50**
  ultraviolet protection 50
  water 50
diarrhoeal disorders 126
disaccharides 115
disciplines, combining 86
dislocations 126
double sea kayak **57**
dry-bags 44
dual-layered socks 40
dynamic rope **68**
Eco-Challenge 9, 10, 11
eddies 59
electrolyte powder **126**
EMA see Expediçao Mata
  Atlantica
Endorphin Fix 10

energy bars 121
environment, respect for 33
equipment 22–23
error recovery 104
Eskimo roll **27**, **59**
Expediçao Mata Atlantica
  146–147
eyewear **39**
Fa'ave, Nathan **12**, **15**
fats 115
fever 127
fibre 118
fibre-glass canoes **56**
figure-8 friction device **68**
first-aid kit **36**, **122**, **131**
fluid imbalances 125
food selection 121
foot care 13, 41
  powder **41**
footwear 40
frostbite **124**
frostnip 124
Fusil, Gérard 9, 12, 13
gaffer tape **36**
Gaimard, Alain 12
gear items, additional 44
gear, biking 35
  boating 35
  climbing 35
  mandatory 35
  medical kit 35
  personal 35
gear, sprint race 17
glacier travel 72
  equipment 72
  hazards 72
  skills 72
glissading 70
Global Extreme Event 132
global postioning system (GPS)
  102
gloves **37**, **74**
Glycaemic Index (GI) 28, 116,
  117
gorges 89
Grand Traverse 13 see also Raid
  Gauloises
Gurney, Steve 15

hard-tail 20, 54
head torch **36**
heat cramps 123
  exhaustion 123
  stroke 123
  syncope 123
helmet 54
High Coast 400 20
High Coast 600 142–143
Hi-Tec Dirty Weekend 16
'hitting the wall' 116 see also
  'bonking'
horseback riding 79
Howard, John **12**, 15
Hunt, Geoff 9, **12**
hybrid kayaks 57
hydration bladder **36**, **125**
hydration pack 20, **60**
hydraulics, or holes 59
hymenoptera 128
hyponatraemia 125
hypothermia 77, 124
ice axe **74**
  boots **74**
illnesses, heat 123
infection 127
inflatable kayak **57**
  raft **57**
in-line (speed) skating **80**
inner sole **40**
Jones, Neil 15
jumaring 66
keepers 59
Kiwi Coast-to-Coast 12
Laczak, Magda **71**
Land Rover G4 Challenge 46
lateral waves 59
leadership 85
lighter **36**
Lomax, Doug 13
Lombardi, Michelle **37**
Lore, Pascale **12**
luminous stick **36**
magnetic deviation 99, 102
Maki-Rautila, Elina 153
Mandatory Equipment List 35
Mandelli, Jim **88**
Mann, Don **10**, 19

map accuracy 100
    contour lines **98**
    co-ordinates 94
    orientation 100
    reading 94
    scale 97
    symbols 95, 98
marine compass **60**
marshes and swamps 89
medical assistance 122
Messner, Reinhold 64
Mild Seven Outdoor Quest 12, 152–153
minerals 119
moisture and cold management 130
monosaccharides 115
mountain bike **23**
mountain biking 52–55
    clothing 54
    equipment 54
    gear **55**
    terrain tips 53
mountain terrain 53
mountain-bike frames 54
mountaineering 64–68
    clothing 68
    equipment 68
    gear and equipment **69**
    skills 66
multi-tasking 93
multi-tool **36**
navigation 22
    board **54**
    techniques 102
    aids 22
navigator's role 104
nutrition 27
Odyssey Adventure Racing 10
open-water swimming 78
Ordnance Survey British Grid (OSBG) 96
Otto, Hano **77**
Otto, Sonja **77**
overtrousers **39**
pack animals **79**
padded shorts **39**
paddles **60**
paddling jacket **60**
    technique 62–63
    tips, watercraft 62

passport control points (PCs) 21, 90–93
Peary, Robert Edwin 8
personal floating device **60, 77**
plastic river kayaks **56**
polysaccharides 115
preparation, mental and physical 26
    race 24
pre-race support 107–108
pre-start support 109
Primal Quest (2003) 15
pronation 40
protein 114, **115**
race briefing 83
    directors 83
Race of Three Sports 9 see also Course des Trois Sports
race organizer's responsibilities 32
race passport 85
race preparations 24
    backup crew 25
    maps 25
    research 24
    route options 24
    weather 25
race safety 31
race support 110
racing skis, classic 70
Raid Blanc event 9, 12
Raid Gauloises 9, 10, 12, 13, 14, 133 see also Grand Traverse
Raid the North Extreme 138–139
rappelling (abseiling) 66
ravines 89
rivers 88–89
rope **36**
route finding 85
    options 103
salty foods 121
scorpion stings 128
Scott, Robert 8
sea boot 89
sea kayak **61**
shadow navigation 88
shell jacket **39**
siphons 59
skating skis 70
skins 71

sleep deprivation 28
    coping 28
sleeping bag **36**
selenium 119
snake bites 128
snowshoes 71
Southern Traverse 11, 12, 15, 150–151
SPD (Shimano Pedalling Dynamics) shoes 54
spider bites 128
sports drinks **117**, 121
sprains 126
standing waves 59
strainers 59
strobe light **36**
Subaru Primal Quest 136–137
sunburn (photodermatitis) 123
sunglasses 60
supplements 119
support crew **93**
support skills, driving 101, 112
    first aid 112
    mechanics 112
    navigation 111
    therapy 112
surgical gloves **122**
survival blanket **36**
    items, basic 30
    tips 30
Swazi Extreme 148–149
Swedish High Coast 400
tactical planning 84
Teams
    Designer Aluminium 13
    Energy **120**
    Hi-Tech 153
    Maybe X-Din (Sweden) **20**, 85
    Mazda/First Ascent 37
    Nike ACG/Balance Bar 29
    Nokia 153
    Odyssey 10
    Salomon (Canada) 70
    Salomon (Poland) **71**
    Subaru (Canada) 70, **88**
    Subaru (USA) **81**
    Subaru 18
team synergy, developing 29
teaming up 21
thermal layering 37, 38, 74, 124

thermodynamic top **39**
throw-line 60
tissue damage 127
topographical maps 25, 83, 94–100
trail shoe design **40**
transition points (TPs) 22, 90
    tips 93
trekking and trail running 47–51
    terrain techniques 48
    canyoning and coasteering 48
    sand 48
    single-track 48
    gear **51**
trekking poles 21, **36**, **77**
tube friction device **68**
Tyrolean traverse 66
Ulansky, Chad 60, 70
Universal Polar Stereographic (UPS) grid 96
Universal Transverse Mercator (UTM) grid 96
vasoconstriction 124
vasodilation 123
vegetation **25**
venomous stings 128
vitamin E 119
vitamins 119
vitamin C 119
water bladders **118**
    hazards 59
    skills 58–59
water sport 56–63
    craft types 56
    carbon fibres 57
    gear and equipment 60, **61**
waterproof socks **37**, **40**
waxed skis 71
waxless skis 71
wetsuit 60
whirlpools 59
whistle **36**
wing paddle **58**
winter clothing 74
winter disciplines 70–76
winter gear 74, **75**
wounds **127**
wrist-top computer **39**
X-Adventure Raid 10
zinc 119
zip wires 66

Acknowledgments

This book must rate as the most difficult I have worked on. Many hours of research, innumerable phone calls beyond the international dateline, hundreds of emails and looming deadlines meant the 'sleep monster' came home to roost for much of 2003. The international nature of the sport makes it impossible to compartmentalize adventure racing and, as can be expected, athletes, organizers and enthusiasts from all over the world pitched in with their opinion on what AR is about.

A special word of thanks must therefore go to the many AR personalities around the globe who selflessly contributed to this book. People like Ian Adamson, Cathy Sassin, Don Mann, Geoff Hunt, Robyn Benincasa, Brian Elliot, Gary Tompsett, Johan Andersson, Trevor Ball, Ugene Nel, Chad Ulansky, David Ogden, Mikael Nordstrom, Nathan Fa'ave and Mark Collins took time out to share tips and check content; it has been a pleasure to work with you all and I sincerely hope you are as satisfied with the end result as I am.

In writing a book as comprehensive as this, it is usually necessary to contract expert writers and/or researchers to cover the many varied and diverse sections. Firstly to Lisa de Speville, my co-author who covered navigation, back-up crews, medical emergencies and nutrition – love your work. Thumbs up also to Ugene Nel who contributed the lion's share on the chapter covering race tactics and strategy, and also to Cathy Sassin for crafting the foreword.

And finally, of course, there are the athletes and race officials at the Desert Challenge, the Africa Adventure Quest, Sweden's High Coast 400, the Arctic Team Challenge and numerous other events. Thank you for tolerating my questions and allowing me to poke my lens into your business on top of mountains, among the dunes, on glaciers and in the swamps. I might not get the chance to race as often as I would like, but sometimes I think covering an AR event comes a very close second to actually taking part. See you out there again soon!

Jacques Marais

Photographic credits